国家出版基金项目
NATIONAL PUBLICATION FOUNDATION

文物与文化遗产篇
Cultural Artifacts and Heritage

汉英对照

中国关键词

KEYWORDS TO UNDERSTAND CHINA

The Palace Museum

故宫

中国外文出版发行事业局（CICG）
故宫博物院（The Palace Museum）
当代中国与世界研究院（ACCWS）
中国翻译研究院（CATL）

朝華出版社
BLOSSOM PRESS

《中国关键词：文物与文化遗产篇——故宫》图书编委会

Editorial Committee

前言

文物与文化遗产是人类文明和智慧的产物，是连接过去与未来的桥梁，承载着各种文明的记忆，诉说着时代的辉煌与变迁。在历史的长河中，中华文明以其深厚的底蕴和独特的魅力，共同构成了人类丰富多彩的文明宝库，其文物与文化遗产数量众多，灿若星辰，是中华民族几千年未曾中断的文化历史的积淀和精华，不仅构筑了中华民族的文化自信，更是全球文明传承与创新的重要力量，为世界文化的多样性和人类文明的交流互鉴提供了宝贵的资源。

为讲好中华优秀传统文化，集中展示中华文明的历史积淀，增进外国受众对中华文化文明的了解，“中国关键词”多语对外传播平台组织策划了《中国关键词：文物与文化遗产篇——故宫》。故宫博物院是在明清紫禁城和宫廷旧藏文物的基础上建立起来的大型综合公共文化机构：既是世界文化遗产，见证了中国六百年兴衰；也是享誉世界的博物馆，其收藏的 186 万余件（套）文物，精品无数，中华民族绵延不断的历史文化在此均能得到充分的印证。本篇按照故宫的责任与理念、宫殿建筑、历代文物精品、宫廷珍宝、文明交流的编写逻辑，在众多顶级文物、文化事件中，优中选优，选取 70 条关键词进行重点解读，向各国读者呈现丰富多彩、生动立体的中华文化形象，推动中华文化更好走向世界。本书为中外对照版，由于篇幅所限，在遴选编写时难免挂一漏万。为使译文更符合目标语读者的阅读习惯，我们对翻译表达进行了创新探索，旨在提升读者的阅读体验。

“中国关键词”多语对外传播平台是中国外文出版发行事业局、当代中国与世界研究院和中国翻译研究院联合实施的国家对外话语创新重点项目，主要围绕新时代中国特色社会主义的理念与实践，进行中文词条专题编写、解读和多语种编译，通过平面、网络、移动端等多媒体、多渠道、多形态持续对外发布，旨在以外国受众易于阅读和理解的方式，阐释中国思想，解读中国理念，传递中国方案，分享中国智慧。

讲故事需要关键词，讲好中国故事需要中国关键词。让我们用“中国关键词”点击中国、沟通世界，促进中外文明交流互鉴。

PREFACE

Cultural artifacts and heritage are the products of human civilization and wisdom, and they serve as a bridge connecting the past and the future. They preserve the memories of various civilizations and narrate the glories and changes of different eras. Throughout its long history, the profound heritage and unique charm of Chinese society have contributed greatly to the rich and colorful treasury of human civilization. Its numerous cultural artifacts and heritage items shine like stars, radiating the accumulation and essence of thousands of years of uninterrupted cultural history of the Chinese nation. Chinese cultural heritage has built cultural confidence among the Chinese people and served as an important force for the inheritance and innovation of global civilization, providing valuable resources for reinforcing the diversity of world cultures and promoting exchange and mutual learning among human civilizations.

Keywords to Understand China: Cultural Artifacts and Heritage—The Palace Museum emerged from the China Keywords program, a multi-language platform to promote international communication. The purpose was to tell stories of fine traditional Chinese culture, showcase the profound heritage of Chinese civilization, and foster better understanding of Chinese culture among foreign readers. The Palace Museum is a large-scale comprehensive cultural institution based on the imperial palace of the Ming (1368-1644) and Qing (1616-1911) dynasties and their collections. It is a World Cultural Heritage site that has witnessed the ups and downs of China over the past six centuries and a world-renowned museum that houses more than 1.86 million pieces (sets) of relics. Its massive collection testifies to the uninterrupted history of Chinese civilization.

Drawing on the outcomes of the Project on the Translation and Communication of the Key Concepts in Chinese Thought and Culture, this book selected 70 keywords to present a vibrant, multi-faceted image of Chinese culture to the world. It narrates the mission and vision of the Palace Museum as well as its palace architecture, relics, royal treasures, and cultural exchange, covering a wide range of rare cultural heritage and milestone cultural events.

The book is bilingual. Due to limited time and space, it is by no means an exhaustive list. We have endeavored to make translation of these keywords easy to understand and idiomatic for readers.

The China Keywords program is a key international communication project launched by the China International Communications Group, the Academy of Contemporary China and World Studies, and the China Academy of Translation. Driven by the concepts and practices of socialism with Chinese characteristics in the new era, program participants edit and translate special Chinese concepts into different languages and release them through multiple printed and online media platforms and channels to interpret Chinese thoughts and ideas and share Chinese solutions and wisdom across linguistic barriers.

Telling a story requires keywords; telling China's story demands distinct keywords intrinsically associated with China. China Keywords are intended to connect China with the rest of the world to promote mutual learning between Chinese and other civilizations.

故宫概览

故宫博物院成立于1925年，是在明清皇宫紫禁城及其丰富收藏基础上建立起来的一座大型综合性博物馆，承载着深厚的历史文化底蕴与民族记忆。它不仅是中国，也是世界上极少数同时具备艺术博物馆、建筑博物馆、历史博物馆、宫廷文化博物馆等特色，并且符合国际公认的“原址保护”“原状陈列”基本原则的著名博物馆。

故宫博物院的两大核心文化资源无疑是其最为宝贵的财富。首先是紫禁城宫殿建筑，这座占地72万平方米的世界文化遗产，拥有千余座保存完好的明清木结构建筑，构成了中国现存规模最大、保存最为完整的古代宫殿建筑群，其雄伟壮观的建筑风貌与精妙绝伦的布局设计，无不彰显着古代中国的建筑智慧与恢宏气魄。

而另一大资源则是其馆藏的186万余件/套珍贵藏品，这些藏品主要源于清宫旧藏，涵盖了书画、陶瓷、玉器、金银器、外国文物等多种类别，每一件都是中华五千年文明史的见证，共同构成了中国古代艺术的璀璨宝库，让后人得以窥见古代社会的风貌与文化的辉煌。

作为故宫世界文化遗产的保护者与管理者，故宫博物院肩负着重要的历史使命。它不仅致力于古建筑与文物的保护与修复工作，还依托这些独特的文化资源，深入研究故宫及其承载的中华优秀传统文化，通过举办多样化的文物及数字展览，创新性地开展公众教育活动，出版学术著作与普及读物，让故宫的文化价值得以广泛传播。同时，故宫博物院还积极与国际社会合作，与英国、法国、意大利、俄罗斯、巴西、伊朗等国家合办中外文化交流展览，共同推动世界多元文明的交流互鉴，使故宫成为全球了解中华文明的一个重要窗口，也为增进各国人民之间的理解和友谊搭建了桥梁。

AN OVERVIEW OF THE PALACE MUSEUM

Founded in 1925, the Palace Museum is a large-scale comprehensive museum established within the Forbidden City, an imperial palace that served the Ming and Qing dynasties and housed their collection of treasures. A carrier of China's profound history, culture, and national memories, it is one of the few museums in the world to integrate arts, architecture, history, and royal culture and a renowned cultural heritage institution that meets the internationally recognized "in-situ preservation" and "in-situ display" principles.

The two core cultural resources of the Palace Museum are undoubtedly its most valuable assets.

The first is the palace architecture of the Forbidden City. A World Cultural Heritage site, the Forbidden City covers an area of 720,000 square meters and consists of over 1,000 wooden-structure buildings from the Ming and Qing dynasties, making it the largest and best-preserved ancient palace complex in China. Its majestic architectural style and exquisite layout design demonstrate the architectural wisdom and grandeur of ancient China.

The second is its collection of more than 1.86 million pieces (sets) of relics. The relics housed in the museum are mostly from the collection of the Qing Dynasty and include calligraphy and paintings, ceramics, jade, gold and silver ware, and imported relics, among many other items. Each is a witness to the 5,000-year history of Chinese civilization, establishing the museum's reputation as the most important treasure house of ancient Chinese arts and allowing future generations a glimpse of the social customs and cultural achievements of ancient China.

As the guardian and manager of this World Cultural Heritage site, the Palace Museum shoulders important historic missions. It is not only committed to the protection and restoration of ancient architecture and relics, but also leverages its abundant resources to study the Forbidden City and the excellent traditional Chinese culture therein. The museum is dedicated to spreading the cultural value of the Forbidden City through organizing a variety of relic exhibitions in both physical and digital forms, carrying out public education activities, and publishing academic works and popular science books. It is also actively promoting international cooperation. The museum has co-organized cultural exchange exhibitions with partners from countries like the UK, France, Italy, Russia, Brazil, and Iran to advance exchange and mutual learning among world civilizations. By doing so, it serves as a significant window for the world to understand Chinese civilization as well as a bridge deepening mutual understanding and friendship between peoples of different countries.

目录

CONTENTS

二

四

太和殿
太和殿

一

故宫的职责和理念

故宫博物院始终秉持“保护第一、加强管理、挖掘价值、有效利用、让文物活起来”的文物工作要求，致力于传承与弘扬中华优秀传统文化。步入新时期，故宫博物院更是明确了办院指导思想，以“平安故宫、学术故宫、数字故宫、活力故宫”建设作为支撑，力求在保护文化遗产的同时，通过学术研究、科技创新与活化利用，让中华优秀传统文化焕发新的生机，为中华文化的国际传播贡献力量。

DUTIES AND PHILOSOPHY

The Palace Museum, upholding the guidelines of "putting protection first while strengthening management, exploring cultural value, promoting effective utilization, and bringing relics to life", is committed to preserving and promoting fine traditional Chinese culture. In the new era, the museum has focused on the principal mission of building a "safe, academic, digital, and dynamic museum". While enhancing the protection of cultural heritage, it has worked to inject new vitality into excellent traditional Chinese culture through academic research, technological innovation, and creative utilization to contribute to the international dissemination of Chinese culture in effective ways.

故宫博物院

故宫博物院成立于 1925 年，是在明清皇宫紫禁城及其收藏基础上建立起来的大型综合性博物馆。

故宫博物院拥有两大文化资源，一是紫禁城宫殿建筑，二是 186 万余件 / 套藏品。紫禁城是世界文化遗产，占地 72 万平方米，拥有千余座明清木结构建筑，是中国现存规模最大、保存最完整的古代宫殿建筑群。藏品主要源于清宫旧藏，包括书画、陶瓷、玉器、金银器、外国文物等多种类别，堪称最重要的中国古代艺术宝库。

故宫全景

A panoramic view of the Palace Museum.

The Palace Museum

Founded in 1925, the Palace Museum is a large-scale comprehensive museum established on the basis of the Forbidden City, an imperial palace for the Ming and Qing dynasties, and their collection of treasures.

The Palace Museum boasts two major cultural resources: the palace architecture of the Forbidden City and a collection of more than 1.86 million pieces (sets) of relics. A World Cultural Heritage site, the Forbidden City covers an area of 720,000 square meters and consists of over 1,000 wooden-structure buildings from the Ming and Qing dynasties, making it the largest and best-preserved ancient palace complex in China. The relics housed in the museum are mostly from the collection of the Qing Dynasty and include calligraphy and paintings, ceramics, jade, gold and silver ware, and imported relics, among many other items, establishing the museum's reputation as the most important treasure house of ancient Chinese arts.

太和门区域

The Gate of Supreme Harmony.

故宫博物院作为故宫世界文化遗产的保护者、管理者，依托丰富的古建筑和文物资源，研究故宫及其承载的中华优秀传统文化，举办多样的文物及数字展览，开展公众教育活动，出版学术著作和普及读物。在向海内外公众展现悠久灿烂的中华文明的同时，也与英国、法国、意大利、俄罗斯、巴西、伊朗等合办中外文化交流展览，共同推动世界多元文明的交流互鉴。

太和门广场

The square in front of the Gate of Supreme Harmony.

As the guardian and manager of this World Cultural Heritage site, the Palace Museum has leveraged its abundant resources of ancient buildings and relics to study the Forbidden City and the excellent traditional Chinese culture therein, organized a variety of relics exhibitions in both physical and digital forms, carried out public education activities, and published academic works and popular science books.

While showcasing time-honored and splendid Chinese civilization to the public at home and abroad, it has also co-organized cultural exchange exhibitions with partners from countries like the UK, France, Italy, Russia, Brazil, and Iran to promote exchange and mutual learning among world civilizations.

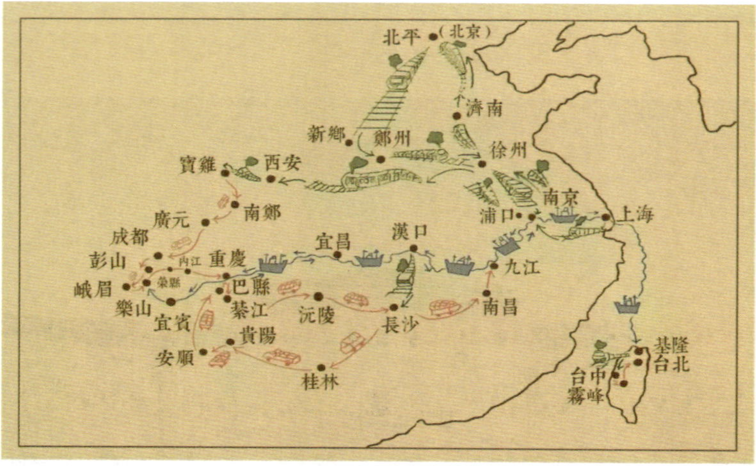

文物南迁路线图

The routes of the southward evacuation of relics.

文物南迁

文物南迁是 20 世纪 30 至 50 年代，故宫博物院、颐和园等单位为躲避战乱，将国宝级文物精品运往南方安全保存的一段历史，可分为南迁、西迁、东归、迁台和北返等多个阶段。

1933 年，约两万箱文物分五批南迁至上海，其中故宫文物 13427 箱又 64 包。1936 年，由上海迁转至南京文物库房。1937 年，抗日战争战事日趋紧张，南迁文物分三路向西南后方迁移，辗转保存于贵阳、重庆、汉中、乐山等地。1945 年，存于西南诸省的文物集中到重庆后东归南京。1948 年，2972 箱文物被运至台湾，现存台北故宫博物院。中华人民共和国成立后，一万余箱南迁文物分三批从南京运回北京，剩余 2221 箱留于南京。

Southward Evacuation of Relics

The southward evacuation of relics refers to the relocation of the national treasures housed in the Palace Museum, the Summer Palace, and other places in Beijing to the southern regions to protect them from warfare from the 1930s to 1950s. The whole process was divided into several phases including southward relocation, westward relocation, east return, relocation to Taiwan, and return to Beijing.

In 1933, about 20,000 boxes of relics were moved south to Shanghai in five waves, including 13,427 boxes and 64 packs from the Palace Museum in Beijing. In 1936, they were relocated from Shanghai to Nanjing. In 1937, with the further escalation of the Chinese People's War of Resistance Against Japanese Aggression, the relics were moved again to southwestern rear areas, such as Guiyang, Chongqing, Hanzhong, and Leshan, along three routes. In 1945, the relics stored in the southwestern regions were transported to Chongqing and then to Nanjing. In 1948, 2,972 boxes of relics were transported to Taiwan, which are now stored in the Palace Museum in Taipei. After the founding of the People's Republic of China in 1949, more than 10,000 boxes of relics evacuated southward were transported back to Beijing from Nanjing in three waves, with the remaining 2,221 boxes kept in Nanjing.

南迁文物在太和门前集中（一）

Relics placed in front of the Gate of Supreme Harmony before their southward evacuation (1).

文物南迁举国合力，历时 15 年、行程上万里，跨越大半个中国 20 多个城市，而约 2 万件文物中没有一件丢失，基本完整保存，堪称世界文化史上的奇迹。其间，部分文物在伦敦、莫斯科、上海、南京等地展出。

文物南迁是伟大的国宝长征，承载着一段深刻隽永的中华民族记忆，是文物工作者为民族历史文化保存写下的时代篇章，创造了人类保护文化遗产的奇迹。

南迁文物在太和门前集中（二）

Relics placed in front of the Gate of Supreme Harmony before their southward evacuation (2).

An endeavor that mobilized nationwide forces and lasted for 15 years, the southward evacuation of relics spanned more than 20 cities, traversing thousands of miles. In the process, none of the some 20,000 relics were lost, and all of them remained basically intact, which is considered a miracle in the history of world culture. During this period, some relics were even exhibited in London, Moscow, Shanghai, Nanjing and other places.

The southward evacuation of relics was a "Long March" of national treasures, representing an episode of history etched in the memory of the Chinese nation, a brilliant chapter written by cultural heritage workers in the preservation of national history and culture, and a miracle of cultural heritage protection for mankind.

太和门
The Gate of Supreme Harmony.

使命与愿景

故宫博物院以真实完整地保护并负责任地传承弘扬故宫承载的中华优秀传统文化作为自己的使命。以将故宫博物院建成国际一流博物馆、世界文化遗产保护的典范、文化和旅游融合的引领者与文明交流互鉴的中华文化会客厅作为自己的愿景。

故宫博物院以习近平新时代中国特色社会主义思想为指导，深入落实“保护第一、加强管理、挖掘价值、有效利用、让文物活起来”的文物工作要求，以“平安故宫、学术故宫、数字故宫、活力故宫”建设为支撑，健全完善故宫博物院管理九大体系，即安防管理体系、文物科技保护体系、学术科研体系、数字故宫体系、开放服务体系、展陈体系、传承转化体系、人才支撑体系和行政保障体系，勇担使命，确保四个愿景的实现。

太和门广场

The square in front of the Gate of Supreme Harmony.

Mission and Vision

The mission of the Palace Museum is to preserve and promote the authenticity and integrity of fine traditional Chinese culture it carries in a responsible manner, with a vision to build the Palace Museum into a world-class institution, a model for cultural heritage protection globally, a pacesetter in the integration of culture and tourism, and a Chinese cultural parlor for exchange and mutual learning among civilizations.

Guided by Xi Jinping Thought on Socialism with Chinese Characteristics for a New Era, the Palace Museum has set guidelines of "putting protection first, strengthening management, exploring cultural value, promoting effective utilization, and bringing relics to life" throughout its operations.

To build a safe, academic, digital, and dynamic museum, the Palace Museum has improved nine management systems: security management, high-tech relics protection, academic research, digital museum services, open services, exhibition organization, inheritance and transformation, talent support, and administrative guarantees. All of these are pointed at ensuring realization of the aforesaid vision.

平安故宫

Building a safe museum.

“四个故宫”理念

故宫博物院于 2019 年正式提出“四个故宫”的概念，意即“平安故宫”“学术故宫”“数字故宫”“活力故宫”。“平安故宫”是基础，“学术故宫”是核心，“数字故宫”是保障，“活力故宫”是追求，“四个故宫”的有序推进及协同发展，是故宫博物院实现使命与愿景的具体路径。

学术故宫

Building an academic museum.

Building a Safe, Academic, Digital, and Dynamic Museum

In 2019, the Palace Museum introduced the idea of building a "safe, academic, digital, and dynamic museum". A "safe museum" is the foundation, an "academic museum" is the core, a "digital museum" is the guarantee, and a "dynamic museum" is the ultimate pursuit. Currently, the Palace Museum is working to turn the idea into reality in an orderly and coordinated manner, which represents the specific path to realize its mission and vision.

“平安故宫”指通过行政管理和科技手段，保障遗产地、文物藏品和观众群体的安全。“学术故宫”指通过学术交流平台、学术团队建设和学术成果发表阵地，吸引国内外专家学者协同推动故宫博物院学术研究向高水平迈进。“数字故宫”指通过对数字技术的利用和数字资源的管理，实现遗产和文物资源的永久保存和永续传承。“活力故宫”指通过挖掘文物蕴含的文化价值，创造性地转化为展览展示活动、文化创意产品、新媒体传播内容等公众文化教育资源，赋予中华优秀传统文化现代表现形式和新的时代内涵。

数字故宫

Building a digital museum.

活力故宫

Building a dynamic museum.

Building a "safe museum" refers to ensuring the security of the cultural heritage site, collection, and visitors in the museum through administrative and technological means.

Building an "academic museum" refers to fostering academic exchange platforms, academic research teams and academic results publishing channels to attract both Chinese and foreign experts to jointly lift the museum's academic research to a higher level.

Building a "digital museum" refers to achieving permanent preservation and sustained inheritance of relic resources through usage of digital technology and management of digital resources.

Building a "dynamic museum" refers to putting a modern face and fresh perspectives on fine traditional Chinese culture by creatively exploring the cultural value of relics and transforming them into public cultural and educational resources through exhibitions, cultural and creative products, and new media content.

太和论坛与会嘉宾合影

Participants of the Taihe Forum pose for a photo in the Palace Museum.

太和论坛

故宫博物院于 2016 年发起“太和·世界古代文明保护论坛”，该论坛是文化遗产领域国际合作交流平台。论坛致力于探讨当今国际环境下世界各地文化遗产保护方面存在的问题，促进文化遗产领域的交流与合作，推动世界古代文明在当今人类社会发展中持续发挥作用。

2016 年 10 月，在首届论坛上，故宫博物院同与会国家及有关国际组织共同发布了《太和宣言》，旨在促进人类文明保护与发展，倡导各国相互尊重、彼此聚合，共筑和谐世界。截至 2023 年年底，论坛已举办六届。共汇集来自中国、埃及、希腊、意大利、印度、伊朗等 20 余个国家的博物馆、科研院所的专家学者的真知灼见，在国际文化遗产保护领域产生了积极广泛的影响。

Taihe Forum

In 2016, the Palace Museum launched the Taihe Forum on Protecting the World's Ancient Civilization as an international exchange and cooperation platform in the field of cultural heritage. The forum is committed to discussing issues concerning cultural heritage preservation around the world, promoting exchange and cooperation in the realm of cultural heritage, and optimizing the role of the world's ancient civilizations in driving the development of human society today.

At the inaugural Taihe Forum in October 2016, the Palace Museum published the *Taihe Declaration* in partnership with participating countries and international organizations, with an aim to promote the protection and development of human civilizations and call for mutual respect and collaboration among countries to build a harmonious world together.

By the end of 2023, the Taihe Forum had been held six times, bringing together insights from experts and scholars from museums and research institutes in more than 20 countries, including China, Egypt, Greece, Italy, India, and Iran, creating a positive, extensive impact on global cultural heritage conservation.

故宫考古

故宫考古是在研究中国古代文明形成、发展与特点的宏观课题下，依托故宫自身优势，致力于与宫廷相关遗存的考古调查及研究。故宫考古结合中国文化遗产保护实际，践行宫廷建筑考古的理念、方法与研究手段，并积极承担和参与重大考古调查发掘项目。

故宫考古以重点推进紫禁城内考古发掘与研究为基础，兼顾各地考古遗址发掘与研究外延，承担和参与凤阳明中都遗址、广汉三星堆遗址、景德镇御窑厂遗址等地的考古发掘工作。

自 2019 年以来，故宫博物院参加了中亚地区“一带一路”考古调查和发掘项目，开展丝绸之路文明交流和中西方文化比较研究；联合英国杜伦大学考古系开展阿联酋拉斯海马考古发掘与研究等工作，拓展国际交流与合作。

故宫考古利用各种形式阐释、传播考古调查发掘和研究成果，推动“学术故宫”建设，发挥考古对故宫事业发展的促进作用。

Archaeology at the Palace Museum

The Palace Museum leverages its advantages to perform dedicated archaeological research on cultural heritage related to royal courts including macro topics of the formation, development and characteristics of ancient Chinese civilization.

In light of the actual conditions of China's cultural heritage protection, the Palace Museum has practiced the concepts, approaches, and research methods for palace architectural archaeology and actively undertaken and participated in major archaeological excavation projects.

Such efforts focused on archaeological excavations and research in the Forbidden City while undertaking and participating in excavations of archaeological sites in various places such as the Ming-dynasty imperial city ruins in Fengyang County, Chuzhou City of east China's Anhui Province, the Sanxingdui site in Guanghan, Chengdu City, capital of southwest China's Sichuan Province, and the imperial kiln ruins in Jingdezhen City, Jiangxi Province, east China.

Since 2019, the Palace Museum has participated in a number of Belt and Road archaeological survey and excavation projects in Central Asia, carrying out exchange between Silk Road civilizations and comparative research on Chinese and Western cultures. It has also cooperated with the Department of Archaeology at Durham University in Britain to conduct archaeological excavation and research on Ras Al Khaimah in the United Arab Emirates, thus expanding international exchange and cooperation.

The Palace Museum employs various forms of media to interpret and disseminate the results of its archaeological investigations, excavations, and studies, accelerating the construction of an "academic museum", and optimizing the role of archaeology in promoting the development of the Palace Museum.

太和学者计划

太和学者计划是故宫博物院推出的国际学术交流项目和人才培养项目，于 2022 年 8 月正式启动，该计划的愿景是减少文明冲突，构建和谐的国际环境。

该计划分为学术来访和学术出访两种形式。学术来访支持国（境）外从事中国历史文化及相关研究的学者到故宫博物院开展交流，旨在引进先进理念与经验，培养了解中华文化的国际学者。学术出访支持故宫博物院学者赴国（境）外开展交流，旨在为故宫学者开拓视野、提升水平，推动故宫博物院科研学术的国际化发展。

太和学者计划借助故宫博物院的资源与人才优势，搭建平等对话、开放合作的国际学术平台，对扩大中华文化影响力、促进文明交流互鉴具有重要意义。

太和学者在进行学术交流

Taihe Scholars conduct academic exchange.

Taihe Scholar Fellowship Program

The Taihe Scholar Fellowship Program, launched by the Palace Museum in August 2022, aims to promote international academic exchange and talent cultivation, with a vision to reduce conflict between civilizations and create a harmonious international environment.

The program is conducted in two forms: inbound academic visits and outbound academic visits.

Inbound academic visits welcome scholars engaged in the research of Chinese history, culture, and other sectors from beyond China to carry out academic exchange at the Palace Museum, aiming to introduce advanced ideas and experience and cultivate international scholars who understand Chinese culture.

Outbound academic visits support Palace Museum scholars to carry out academic exchange abroad, aiming to broaden the horizons and enhance the capabilities of those scholars and promote the internationalized development of the Palace Museum's scientific and academic research.

Leveraging the Palace Museum's resource and talent advantages, the program is committed to building an international academic exchange platform featuring equal dialogue, openness, and cooperation, and plays a significant role in expanding the global influence of Chinese culture and promoting exchange and mutual learning among civilizations.

优化升级后的垃圾桶

Upgraded trash bins in the Palace Museum.

故宫零废弃

2020 年 1 月，故宫博物院与万科公益基金会联合发起“故宫零废弃”项目，旨在通过科学精细的废弃物管理方式，提高资源利用效率，倡导公众响应气候变化行动，将故宫博物院建设为国际领先的零废弃博物馆。

该项目分为“零废弃办公”和“零废弃游览”两个阶段，以减量化、资源化、无害化为原则，按阶段推进。对内建设阶段，采集并分析观众环境行为数据，完成垃圾桶点位优化及外观升级，结合故宫景观建设生态堆肥花坛，并向故宫员工进行培训。对外倡导阶段，展示由故宫回收废弃物创作而成的雕塑作品，

"福牛辞旧"废弃物再生雕塑

An ox sculpture made of recycled waste.

Zero Waste in the Palace Museum

In January 2020, the Palace Museum joined hands with the Vanke Foundation to launch a zero-waste campaign, aiming to build a world-leading waste-free museum through adopting a science-based and meticulous approach to waste management, maximizing resource utilization efficiency and increasing public awareness of the response to climate change.

The campaign was divided into two stages: zero-waste office and zero-waste tours, which have been proceeding in a phased manner to promote waste reduction, recycling, and pollution-free treatment.

Internally, the Palace Museum has optimized the locations and appearances of trash bins based on analysis of data on visitors' environmental behavior, built eco-friendly composts for flower beds according to the landscape layout of the Forbidden City, and strengthened relevant training of staff members.

Externally, the museum advocates environmental protection among visitors through presenting zero-waste cultural and creative

光盘行动的海报

A poster promoting the "empty plate" campaign.

推出零废弃文创产品、科普图文及视频，开展光盘行动、零废弃导览等公众活动。2023 年，该项目亮相于第二十八届联合国气候变化大会，向世界生动展示中国文旅文博行业绿色低碳发展成果。

"故宫零废弃"是故宫博物院践行绿色发展理念的重要举措，将会有助于讲好中国博物馆绿色故事，打造"红墙绿景"新名片，在节能减排、理念倡导方面为社会做出积极贡献。

生态堆肥花坛旁的堆肥箱和蚯蚓塔

Compost bin and worm tower beside an ecological flower bed.

products as well as environmental brochures and videos and launching the "empty plate" campaign, zero-waste guided tours, and other activities.

In 2023, the zero-waste campaign of the Palace Museum was exhibited as an innovative practice at the COP28 UN Climate Change Conference, vividly showcasing the contributions made by China's culture, tourism, and museum sectors to green, low-carbon development worldwide.

The zero-waste campaign is an important measure of the Palace Museum to practice a green development philosophy. It has helped tell green development stories of Chinese museums, create a new calling card for the Palace Museum featuring "red walls and a green environment", and promote concepts of energy conservation and emission reduction throughout society.

二

宫殿建筑文化

故宫，作为中国古代宫殿建筑的典范，其营建理念深植于悠久的传统文化土壤之中，沿袭了“天人合一”“中轴对称”等古制，建筑类型从巍峨的殿堂到精致的亭台楼阁，应有尽有，构成了一幅宏大的古代建筑画卷。这些建筑不仅展现了古代工匠的智慧与技艺，更深刻体现了中华文明中严整均衡的礼序传承和“守中致和”的哲学思维，每一砖一瓦都诉说着历史的沧桑与文化的厚重，是中华文明源远流长的重要物质载体。

PALACE ARCHITECTURE

The Palace Museum, also known as the Forbidden City, is an exemplary model of ancient Chinese palace architecture. Deeply rooted in the soil of long-standing traditional Chinese culture, its architecture follows ancient design concepts such as "unity of heaven and man" and "symmetry along a central axis" and includes many building types ranging from magnificent palaces and halls to exquisite pavilions. These structures compose a grand picture of classical Chinese architecture, not only manifesting the wisdom and skills of ancient craftsmen, but also embodying the strict, balanced etiquette inheritance and the philosophical thinking of "keeping the middle and achieving harmony" in Chinese civilization.

紫禁城雪景

The Forbidden City after snow.

紫禁城

紫禁城落成于1420年，由明朝第三位皇帝朱棣修建。作为明清两代的皇宫，先后有24位皇帝在此居住，统治中国长达491年。

紫禁城之名源于紫微垣，即北极星所在。古人认为它永悬于中天，是天帝居所。皇帝自称天子，所居也应取“紫”字象征中央，又因皇室禁地不可擅入，故名“紫禁城”。1912年清王朝灭亡，紫禁城作为曾经的皇宫，称“故宫”。

紫禁城平面大致呈长方形，南北961米，东西753米，占地约72万平方米。四面城墙各开一门，城墙四角各有角楼。城内建筑沿南北中轴线向两侧展开，依照礼制与功用形成对称布

紫禁城午门

The Meridian Gate of the Forbidden City.

The Forbidden City

The Forbidden City, completed in 1420, was built by Zhu Di, the third emperor of the Ming Dynasty. It served as the imperial palace of the Ming and Qing dynasties. A total of 24 emperors lived here while ruling China for 491 years.

The Forbidden City ("*Zijincheng*" in Chinese, literally meaning "Purple Forbidden City") derived its name from Purple Forbidden Enclosure ("*Ziweiyuan*" in Chinese), where the North Star is located. The ancient Chinese believed that it would hang forever in the middle of heaven and was the residence of the Emperor of Heaven. The emperor called himself the "son of heaven", and his residence was named with "purple" to symbolize the center.

People were not allowed to enter without permission, so the imperial palace was literally called "Purple Forbidden City". After the fall of the Qing Dynasty in 1912, the Forbidden City, the former imperial palace, transformed into the Palace Museum.

The layout of the Forbidden City strictly followed the architectural norms recorded in *The Rites of Zhou—Artificers' Record*, which is known as "five gates, three courts, and nine heavens". The Forbidden City roughly has a rectangular layout and extends 961 meters from north to south and 753 meters from east to west, with an area of 720,000 square meters. Each of its four

局。南部为外朝，以太和殿、中和殿、保和殿为中心，是皇帝举行重要活动的朝政区。北部为内廷，以乾清宫、交泰殿、坤宁宫为中心，并建有御花园，是帝后嫔妃的生活区。

紫禁城营建理念沿袭古制，建筑类型复杂多样，集中国古代建筑文化之大成，展现了“天人合一”“阴阳”“五行五色”等思想理念，是中国古代官式建筑的最高典范。

太和门广场

The square in front of the Gate of Supreme Harmony.

walls has a gate, and there is a corner tower at each of the four corners.

The buildings in the Forbidden City are distributed along a north-south axis, forming a symmetrical layout according to the ritual system and their functions.

The southern part is the outer court, with the Hall of Supreme Harmony (*Taihe dian*), the Hall of Middle Harmony (*Zhonghe dian*), and the Hall of Preserving Harmony (*Baohe dian*) at the center. It was where the emperor held courts and important ceremonies.

The northern part is the inner court, with the Palace of Heavenly Purity (*Qianqing gong*), the Hall of Union (*Jiaotai dian*), and the Palace of Earthly Tranquility (*Kunning gong*) at the core. Also nearby is the Imperial Garden (*Yuhuayuan*). It was the living area of the emperor, empress, and imperial consorts.

The architectural designs of the Forbidden City followed the ancient system. Featuring diverse types of buildings, it represents the culmination of ancient Chinese architectural culture and showcases the philosophical concepts of "the unity of nature and humans", "*yin* and *yang*" and "five elements and five colors". The Forbidden City is the supreme example of official ancient Chinese architecture.

午门

中国古代，“午”代表正午、正南。以“午”命名的午门，即紫禁城的正南门。

午门平面呈“凹”字形，中部为正楼，两侧为向南延伸的雁翅楼。从南往北看，中间墩台有三个门洞；从北望南看，则是五个门洞，即所谓的“明三暗五”。午门中门洞专供皇帝出入。在清代，皇后大婚当天可通过中门入宫。殿试前三名高中后可从中门出宫，这是天子赐予的无上殊荣。其余四个门洞，东侧大门供高级官员出入，西侧大门供宗室王公出入，左右两个掖门则供三品以下官员和殿试考生行走。午门“进”“出”的盛大仪礼，反映着“齐家”“治国”等中华传统文化理念。

午门也用于举办重要典礼。清代，农历十月初一，皇帝在此举办“颁朔礼”，颁布的历书对于指导农时农耕至关重要。遇战争获胜，在此举行“受俘礼”，奖励功臣，宣扬国威。举办大朝会时，午门钟鼓齐鸣，门洞齐开，车架、宝象等陈于路侧，十分隆重。

午门作为最大且最为壮观的城门，充分展现出紫禁城的皇家威仪与庄严肃穆。

The Meridian Gate (*Wu Men*)

In Chinese culture, "Meridian" represents noon and the south. Thus, the Meridian Gate is the south gate of the Forbidden City.

The Meridian Gate features a concave layout and consists of a main building in the middle and two wings that extend southwards. Looking from south to north, one can see three doorways in the middle tower; viewed from north to south, the middle tower has five doorways. The Meridian Gate stands on the central axis of the Forbidden City.

The central doorway was for exclusive use by the emperor in the Ming and Qing dynasties. However, an empress was granted the privilege of using this doorway once, and only once, on her wedding day during the Qing Dynasty. As a special honor granted by the emperor, the three best-performing candidates in the Palace Examination, the highest level of the imperial examinations, would be permitted to leave the imperial palace through the central doorway after their interview with the emperor.

The smaller door to the east was used by high-ranking officials while that to the west was used by the royal family. The remaining two doorways at the corners were used by lower-ranking officials and candidates attending the Palace Examination.

The strict rules of etiquette concerning the use of the Meridian Gate in ancient times reflect traditional Chinese cultural concepts such as "family management" and "state governance".

The Meridian Gate was also a venue for important ceremonies. In the Qing Dynasty, the emperor held a ceremony here to issue the next year's calendar on the 1st day of the tenth lunar month, which played a vital role in guiding agricultural activities. When the army returned in triumph after wars, the emperor received the captives and rewarded meritorious warriors at the Meridian Gate to promote national prestige.

The bells and drums at the Meridian Gate sounded together when grand ceremonies were held in the Hall of Supreme Harmony. On such occasions, all doorways were open, and chariots, elephant sculptures, and other ceremonial instruments lined the passage, creating a solemn atmosphere.

The Meridian Gate is the biggest and most magnificent gate of the Forbidden City, reflecting royal authority and the solemnity of the former imperial palace. It is a significant historical site and cultural heritage that witnessed the vicissitudes of feudal China and a cultural symbol that carries profound historical memories.

太和殿内景
Inside the Hall of Supreme Harmony.

太和殿

太和殿俗称“金銮殿”，位于紫禁城中轴线的显要位置，是紫禁城中规模最大、等级最高的宫殿，气度恢宏，威严壮观。

大殿建于明初 1420 年，原称奉天殿，清顺治时改为太和殿。“太和”出自典籍《周易》，表明中华文化崇尚天道自然，崇尚和谐统一。历史上，太和殿曾数度焚毁并重建。作为紫禁城三大殿之首，它与中和、保和二殿共同坐落于三层台基之上，通高 35.05 米。建筑细节和室内陈设，均体现其崇高地位：檐角设 10 个脊兽，数量最多，为全国孤例；檐下绘金龙和玺彩画，等级最高，为宫廷特有；殿内置皇帝宝座，髹（在器物涂

太和殿外景

Outside the Hall of Supreme Harmony.

The Hall of Supreme Harmony (*Taihe Dian*)

The Hall of Supreme Harmony, also known as the Hall of Golden Chimes, occupies the most prominent position on the north-south axis of the Forbidden City. The largest and highest-level building in the Forbidden City, it is magnificent and mighty.

First built in 1420 during the early Ming Dynasty, it was initially named the Hall of Venerating Heaven (*Fengtian dian*) and renamed the Hall of Supreme Harmony during the reign of Emperor Shunzhi (1643-1661) of the Qing Dynasty. Its name "Taihe" comes from *The Book of Changes*, representing the Chinese philosophy of respecting nature and advocating harmony and unity.

Historically, the Hall of Supreme Harmony underwent destruction and reconstruction several times. As the top of the three main halls in the Forbidden City, the 35.05-meter-tall hall sits on a three-tier marble terrace alongside the Hall of Middle Harmony and the Hall of Preserving Harmony.

The architectural details and interior furnishings all reflect its

太和殿屋檐脊兽

Ridge beasts on the roof of the Hall of Supreme Harmony.

漆）金雕龙，为明代遗物。明清两朝，皇帝登基、大婚等重大仪式，均在太和殿举行，另外冬至、元旦、万寿节（即皇帝生日）三大节庆典也必设在太和殿。

太和殿建筑规制之高，装饰手法之精，堪列中国古代建筑之首。作为紫禁城最重要的宫殿，太和殿讲究秩序、重视礼仪、追求和谐，不仅在建筑规模和装饰工艺上展现了中国古代建筑的精华，也承载了许多中国皇室的重要仪式和活动，具有极高的历史和文化价值。

太和殿屋檐下的金龙和玺彩绘

Golden dragon patterns under the eaves of the Hall of Supreme Harmony.

lofty status: Ten mythical animal figurines guard the roof ridges of the Hall of Supreme Harmony, the only example in the country; golden dragon colored paintings are found under the eaves, which were exclusive to the imperial palace; inside the hall is the imperial throne painted and carved with golden dragons, which can be traced back to the Ming Dynasty.

In the Ming and Qing dynasties, the emperor's enthronement, weddings, and other major ceremonies were held in the Hall of Supreme Hall. Celebrations for the Winter Solstice, the Chinese New Year, and the emperor's birthday also took place here.

The Hall of Supreme Harmony ranks first among the ancient Chinese buildings in terms of architectural standards and decoration techniques.

As the most important structure in the Forbidden City, the architectural designs of the Hall of Supreme Harmony focus on order, etiquette, and harmony. With extremely high historical and cultural value, it not only displays the essence of ancient Chinese architecture in architectural scale and decoration methods, but has also witnessed many important ceremonies and activities of the royal family in ancient China.

保和殿外景

Outside the Hall of Preserving Harmony.

保和殿

保和殿是故宫外朝三大殿之一，从明至清，名称多次改易。顺治皇帝居住时称“位育宫”，大婚亦在此举行。康熙皇帝也曾在此居住，称“清宁宫”。

明初，这里称“谨身殿”，是皇帝举行大典前更换礼服的场所。清朝每年除夕和正月十五，皇帝在保和殿内宴请新疆、蒙古等的少数民族王公及公主额驸等，以示重视。

清代，乾隆皇帝将这里作为殿试场所。殿试是科举考试最高级别的考试，皇帝亲自主持，考中者称“天子门生”。殿试前三名为状元、榜眼、探花，可享受从午门中央门洞出宫的殊荣。

保和殿内景

Inside the Hall of Preserving Harmony.

The Hall of Preserving Harmony (*Baohe Dian*)

The Hall of Preserving Harmony is one of the three main halls in the outer court of the Forbidden City. During the Ming and Qing dynasties, it was renamed several times. When Emperor Shunzhi lived here, it was called Weiyu Palace, and the emperor's wedding was held here. Emperor Kangxi also lived here when it was called Qingning Palace.

In the early Ming Dynasty, it was called Jinshen Hall, where the emperor changed ritual clothes before grand ceremonies. During the Qing Dynasty, on Chinese New Year's Eve and the Lantern Festival, the emperor held a banquet in the Hall of Preserving Harmony to entertain princes and princesses of ethnic minorities such as the Uygurs and the Mongolians.

In the Qing Dynasty, Emperor Qianlong used the hall as the venue for the Palace Examination. As the highest level of the imperial examinations, the Palace Examination was presided over by the emperor, and those who passed were called "the emperor's protégés". The top three in the Palace Examination, called Zhuangyuan, Bangyan, and Tanhua, respectively, were granted the privilege to leave the imperial palace through the central doorway of the Meridian Gate.

保和殿后有宫中最大的石雕，长 16 米多，宽 3 米余，厚达 1.7 米，重近 200 吨，由一整块石头雕成。为将此石从七八十公里外运至京城，需要先修路，再每隔一段路挖一口井，冬天从井中取水泼洒成冰，再由人力、骡马在冰面上拖运，仅运输即用 28 天。石上雕海水江崖及九条腾龙，体现了高超的建筑石刻技术，极具艺术观赏价值。

保和殿后大石雕

The magnificent stone carving behind the Hall of Preserving Harmony.

Behind the Hall of Preserving Harmony is the largest stone carving in the Forbidden City, which measures 16 meters in length, 3 meters in width, 1.7 meters in thickness, and nearly 200 tons in weight. It was carved from a whole stone. To transport this gigantic stone from a quarry 70 to 80 kilometers from the capital, people first built a road, and then dug wells at intervals along every other section of the road. That winter, they took water from the wells and splashed it on the road, and then hauled the stone on the iced road by manpower, mules, and horses. It took 28 days to transport the stone to the imperial palace. The stone carving with seawater, cliffs, and nine dragons reflects the superb sculpture technology and has remarkable artistic value.

乾清宫

乾清宫是紫禁城内廷后三宫之一，明清两朝曾多次重修。

这里自明代至清初一直是皇帝寝宫，清代雍正皇帝即位后，移居到西侧养心殿。乾清宫则用于元旦等重要节日举行宴会。康熙、乾隆皇帝曾在此举行千叟宴，宴请年长臣民，以示尊老。皇帝去世后，灵柩停放于此，象征寿终正寝。乾清宫外东西两侧，各有一座高大的石台，台上分别置铜鎏金江山、社稷亭，象征江山永固、社稷长安。

乾清宫外景

Outside the Palace of Heavenly Purity.

The Palace of Heavenly Purity (*Qianqing Gong*)

The Palace of Heavenly Purity is one of the three main palaces in the inner court of the Forbidden City. It was reconstructed several times during the Ming and Qing dynasties.

From the Ming Dynasty to the early Qing time, it served as the emperor's dwelling palace. After Emperor Yongzheng (1723-1735) of the Qing Dynasty ascended the throne, he lived in the Hall of Mental Cultivation (*Yangxin dian*), and the Palace of Heavenly Purity began to be used for banquets on important festivals such as the Chinese New Year. Emperors Kangxi and Qianlong once held banquets here to entertain seniors to show respect for the elderly.

After the death of the emperor, his coffin was laid here, symbolizing a peaceful death. There is a tall stone platform on the eastern and western sides of the Palace of Heavenly Purity, respectively, on which is a gilt copper pavilion that symbolizes everlasting rule and national peace.

乾清宫内悬挂“正大光明”匾。清代自雍正帝开始实行“秘密立储”，即皇帝在位期间，写下继承人的名字，一式两份，一份随身携带，另一份则藏于正大光明匾后。皇帝临终或突然去世后，由大臣当众取出匾后诏书，两份核对无误，方可宣布皇位继承者。

乾清宫作为紫禁城内廷最重要的宫殿，采用重檐庑殿顶，檐角脊兽 9 只，等级仅次于太和殿。

乾清宫内景

Inside the Palace of Heavenly Purity.

Inside the palace, a plaque hangs engraved with four Chinese characters," 正大光明 ", which mean "Justice and Brightness".

From the time of Emperor Yongzheng, the name of the crown prince would be written on two imperial edicts in duplicate. A copy would be kept by the emperor himself, and the other would be placed in a box behind this plaque. Only if the names on the two edicts were verified to be the same would the designated prince take the crown upon the death of the emperor.

As the most important building in the inner court of the Forbidden City, the Palace of Heavenly Purity features a double-eave hip roof and nine mythical animals on each corner ridge, surpassed only by the Hall of Supreme Harmony.

坤宁宫西间

The western chamber of the Palace of Earthly Tranquility.

坤宁宫

坤宁宫始建于明代初年，为皇后寝宫。清代初年改建后，东侧为皇帝大婚的洞房，西侧为祭神场所。

康熙、同治、光绪三位幼年登基的皇帝，大婚洞房即在坤宁宫，末代皇帝溥仪的婚礼洞房也在这里。如今洞房按光绪皇帝大婚场景布置，红色基调，喜床上的被子绣百子图，褥子绣龙凤双喜，床正中放有宝瓶，瓶内盛装金、银、珍珠等物，寓意国泰民安、多子多孙。

坤宁宫西间，是萨满教祭祀的重要场所。每天早晚都有祭祀，不仅有诵神歌，还有乐器伴奏。祭祀时食用仅以白水煮制的猪肉，皇帝还会将肉分赐给王公大臣，但不少人并不喜食这样寡淡无味的食物。

The Palace of Earthly Tranquility (*Kunning Gong*)

The Palace of Earthly Tranquility was built in the early Ming Dynasty as the empress' dwelling palace. After reconstruction in the early Qing Dynasty, the eastern side of the palace served as the bridal chamber on the emperor's wedding day, and the western side was used to worship deities.

Kangxi, Tongzhi, and Guangxu, three Qing-dynasty emperors who ascended the throne at an early age, all made the Palace of Earthly Tranquility their nuptial chamber, as did Puyi, the last emperor of the Qing Dynasty.

Today, the chamber retains the furnishings from when it served as the nuptial chamber for Emperor Guangxu. With red as the main tone, the quilt on the bed is embroidered with the image of a hundred children playing, and the mattress is embroidered with the auspicious patterns of dragons and phoenixes. There is a treasure bottle in the middle of the bed, which contains gold, silver, pearls and other treasures, symbolizing a prosperous country, a peaceful life for the people, and fertile offspring.

The western chamber of the Palace of Earthly Tranquility was a major place for shamanic sacrifices during the Qing Dynasty. Every morning and evening, sacrificial ceremonies were held here, accompanied by chanting of sacred songs and instrumental music.

During a sacrificial ceremony, the emperor only ate boiled pork without any seasoning, and he would also reward princes and ministers with the meat, but few liked to eat such bland and tasteless food.

坤宁宫外景

Outside the Palace of Earthly Tranquility.

不同于紫禁城中轴线上的其他建筑，为萨满祭祀考虑，坤宁宫的门并不居中，而是偏东，窗户采用直棂吊搭式窗，体现出明显的满汉融合建筑风格。

皇帝大婚洞房

The nuptial chamber for the emperor.

Unlike other buildings on the central axis of the Forbidden City, the door of the Palace of Earthly Tranquility is not in the middle, but slightly to the east for the sake of shamanistic sacrifices. The palace also features mullioned hanging windows, showing a distinctive architectural style fusing Manchu and Han elements.

钦安殿

钦安殿为紫禁城御花园中的主体建筑，里面供奉道教水神玄武大帝，是中轴线上为数不多的从未遭受火灾的明代建筑。

明代嘉靖皇帝笃信道教，常于钦安殿举行道教仪式。嘉靖十四年（1535）钦安殿周围增设围墙，形成独立院落，南端正中加盖“天一门”，取自《易经》“天一生水”，与殿内供奉的水神相呼应。门外立有一对獬豸，据传专噬奸佞之人，守护着这座宗教殿堂。

天一门外景

Outside the Gate of Heaven's Primacy.

The Hall of Imperial Peace (*Qin'an Dian*)

The Hall of Imperial Peace is the main building in the Imperial Garden of the Forbidden City. Built to worship Lord Xuanwu, the god of water in Taoism, it is one of the few Ming-dynasty buildings on the central axis that has never suffered a fire.

Emperor Jiajing of the Ming Dynasty believed in Taoism and often held Taoist ceremonies in the Hall of Imperial Peace. In 1535, a wall was added around the hall, forming an independent courtyard. The Gate of Heaven's Primacy (*Tianyi men*) was built in the south, which derived its name from the sentence "Tianyi gives birth to water" in *The Book of Changes*, echoing with the god of water enshrined in the hall. Guarding the outside of the door are a pair of Xiezhi, a mythical animal believed to have the ability to judge between right and wrong and wipe out the wicked by biting or goring them.

钦安殿殿顶

The roof of the Hall of Imperial Peace.

钦安殿殿顶为罕见的重檐盝顶，即由四条脊围合而成的平顶，屋顶中间有铜胎鎏金宝瓶，内藏经书。殿中供奉的玄武大帝，也是掌管北方之神。“玄”即黑色，在五行中对应水，北方亦属水。紫禁城中多为木结构建筑，防火至关重要，御花园中心供奉水神，体现了对大自然的敬畏、对平安美好的祈盼。

钦安殿内供奉的铜鎏金玄武大帝神像

The gilded copper statue of Lord Xuanwu enshrined in the Hall of Imperial Peace.

The Hall of Imperial Peace features a rare type of roof known as *luding*, a flat roof surrounded by four ridges. A gilt copper treasure bottle is in the middle of the roof, which contains scriptures.

Lord Xuanwu enshrined in the hall is the god in charge of the north. *Xuan*, meaning "black", stands for water in the Five Elements, so the north corresponds to water in Chinese culture.

Most of the buildings in the Forbidden City are composed of wood, so fire prevention was crucial. Enshrining the god of water in the center of the Imperial Garden reflected ancient reverence for nature and hope for peace and good fortune.

中正仁和殿

Zhongzheng Renhe Hall.

养心殿

康熙年间，养心殿曾是专门制作宫廷御用物品之处。雍正皇帝把这里改为寝宫后，共有八位皇帝在此居住和处理政务。

养心殿为工字形建筑，前殿、后殿以穿堂相连，且是紫禁城中第一个装上玻璃的宫殿。前殿中间为中正仁和殿，用于召见朝臣、议商政务。东暖阁西南部安装有整片的大玻璃窗，因光线充足敞亮，称为“明窗”。皇帝每年正月初一零时在此“明窗开笔”，书吉语数字，祈祷一年平顺。清晚期“垂帘听政”即在东暖阁，在同治、光绪帝尚年幼时，政务由坐在黄纱帘后的两宫皇太后裁决。

养心殿东暖阁内垂帘听政

The East Warmth Chamber of the Hall of Mental Cultivation, where empress dowagers attended to state affairs behind a yellow curtain in the late Qing Dynasty.

The Hall of Mental Cultivation (*Yangxi Dian*)

During the reign of Emperor Kangxi of the Qing Dynasty, the Hall of Mental Cultivation was used to produce items used by the royal family. After Emperor Yongzheng converted this place into his bedchamber, a total of eight emperors lived and handled government affairs here.

The Hall of Mental Cultivation has a horizontal H-shaped layout, with its front and rear halls connected by a corridor. It was also the first palace in the Forbidden City to be equipped with glass windows.

In the middle of the front hall is Zhongzheng Renhe Hall, where the emperor met ministers to discuss government affairs. In the southwest of the East Warmth Chamber is a large glass window, which is called the "bright window" because of the abundant sunlight. At 0:00 a.m. on the 1st day of the first lunar month each year, the emperor held a ceremony called "opening the pen by the bright window" to write auspicious words and numbers, praying for good luck in the new year. In the late Qing Dynasty, empress dowagers attended to state affairs behind a yellow curtain in the East Warmth Chamber, when Emperors Tongzhi and Guangxu were still young.

西侧有皇帝批阅奏折、与大臣密谈的勤政亲贤殿。最西侧则是乾隆皇帝的书房三希堂和长春书屋。三希堂仅 4 平方米，因乾隆皇帝钟爱的三幅著名稀世书法作品而得名。后殿是皇帝寝宫，两侧为后妃随居之所。

养心殿作为雍正以后的政治权力中心，见证了乾隆盛世，也目睹了清的由盛转衰。

养心殿外景

Outside the Hall of Mental Cultivation.

On the western side is Qinzheng Qinxian Hall, where the emperor read and approved memorials submitted by officials and discussed important affairs with ministers. On the westernmost side are the studies of Emperor Qianlong—the Cabinet of Three Rare Treasures (*Sanxi tang*) and the Study of Everlasting Spring (*Changchun shuwu*).

With an area of only four square meters, the Cabinet of Three Rare Treasures was so named because of the three precious calligraphic works collected by Emperor Qianlong here. The rear hall was the emperor's bedroom, and the chambers on both sides were where imperial consorts resided.

As the center of political power since the period of Emperor Yongzheng, the Hall of Mental Cultivation witnessed both the flourishing age of Emperor Qianlong and the dynasty's gradual decline during subsequent reigns.

文华殿

明初，文华殿落成，宫殿屋顶用绿色琉璃瓦，门前石雕用“三元纹”，即象征太子身份的三团祥云。嘉靖十五年（1536）改为皇帝便殿，覆黄瓦沿用至今。

文华殿是举行“经筵”的场所。经筵，是指皇帝与有学问的大臣共同研读四书五经，于明代正统年间形成规制。经筵以外，文华殿还举行日讲，君臣之间探讨治国理政之道。

The Hall of Literary Brilliance (*Wenhua Dian*)

The Hall of Literary Brilliance, built in the early Ming Dynasty, was originally where the crown prince lived. Back then, it was roofed with green-glazed tiles, with a stone carving of three auspicious clouds in front of the door, a symbol of the crown prince's status in ancient times. In 1536, it began to serve as Emperor Jiajing's temporary dwelling palace, with its roof redone in yellow-glazed tiles, which have been retained to this day.

The Hall of Literary Brilliance was where the emperor studied the Four Books (namely, *The Great Learning*, *The Doctrine of the Mean*, *The Analects of Confucius*, and *The Mencius*) and Five Classics (*The Book of Changes*, *The Book of Songs*, *The Book of Rites*, *The Book of History*, and *Spring and Autumn Annals*) with knowledgeable ministers. This evolved into a routine during Emperor Zhengtong's reign of the Ming Dynasty. The emperor also daily met ministers here to discuss state affairs.

乾隆年间，文华殿后建文渊阁，用于收藏中国古代最大的丛书《四库全书》。文渊阁作为藏书楼，覆黑瓦。黑色对应五行中的“水”，以期为藏书楼克火。因此，在文渊阁及附近区域，随处可见海水、荷花、水草等纹饰，石雕栏板上还有乌龟、螃蟹、鱼虾等，金水河也从阁前流过。凡此种种，皆取水能灭火之意。

文华殿是天子文经天地的象征，也昭示着中华文化重视经典、笃学不倦的历史传统。

文渊阁

The Belvedere of Literary Profundity.

During the period of Emperor Qianlong, the Belvedere of Literary Profundity (*Wenyuan ge*) was built behind the Hall of Literary Brilliance to store the largest book series in ancient China—*The Complete Library of the Four Branches of Literature*.

A building functioning as a library, the Belvedere of Literary Profundity is covered with black tiles because the color black corresponds to water in the Five Elements. This design represents a prayer to protect the library from fires.

Water-related decorative elements such as seawater, lotus, and aquatic weeds can be seen everywhere here, and the stone-carved balustrades are adorned with patterns like tortoises, crabs, fish and shrimp. The Golden Water River also flows in front of the building. All of these convey the idea that water extinguishes fires.

The Hall of Literary Brilliance, a symbol of the imperial court's high esteem for cultural cultivation, manifests the Chinese tradition of attaching importance to classics and education.

武英殿

明初，武英殿是皇帝召见大臣及参加祭祀前斋戒居住的场所。明末农民军领袖李自成攻入紫禁城后，在武英殿登基，但第二天便被迫撤出北京。清初，武英殿成为摄政王多尔衮处理政务的场所。康熙八年（1669），因皇帝寝宫维修，康熙皇帝也曾在此短暂居住。

康熙十九年（1680），清廷在武英殿设立“修书处”。此后，这里作为皇家出版所，大量官方图书在此校勘、印装，称“殿本”。殿本图书不少采用活字印刷，工艺精湛，版式考究。皇帝将图书陈设于书房，或作为礼物赏赐大臣。末代皇帝溥仪退位后，民国政府于 1914 年成立古物陈列所，武英殿成为陈列室，展示来自沈阳、承德等处的宫廷珍宝。

武英殿现为陶瓷馆，常年展出历代陶瓷精品文物，呈现中国作为瓷器大国的悠久历史和传承不断的陶瓷文化。

The Hall of Martial Valor (*Wuying Dian*)

In the early Ming Dynasty, the Hall of Martial Valor was where the emperor summoned ministers and practiced abstinence before sacrificial ceremonies.

At the end of the Ming Dynasty, Li Zicheng, a peasant rebel leader, captured the Forbidden City and ascended the throne at the Hall of Martial Valor. However, he was forced to retreat from Beijing the next day.

In the early Qing Dynasty, the hall became the place where Regent Dorgon handled government affairs. In 1669, Emperor Kangxi lived here for a short time when his dwelling palace was under maintenance.

In 1680, the Qing court set up an office responsible for compiling and publishing books at the Hall of Martial Valor. From then on, it served as a royal publishing house, and many official books were collated and printed here, known as "palace editions".

Many of the palace editions were printed in movable types, with exquisite craftsmanship and design. Emperor Kangxi displayed the books in his study or gave them as gifts to his ministers.

After the abdication of the last emperor Puyi, the government of the Republic of China (1912-1949) established an antiquities exhibition hall in 1914, and the Hall of Martial Valor became a showroom for royal treasures from Shenyang, Chengde, and other places.

The Hall of Martial Valor now serves as the ceramics gallery in the Palace Museum to display porcelain masterpieces from various eras, showcasing the long history and brilliant ceramic culture of China as a key porcelain producer globally.

御花园

御花园位于紫禁城中轴线最北侧，占地 12000 平方米，是紫禁城中最大的花园，供明清帝后妃嫔休闲娱乐所用。

花园中建筑星罗棋布。主体建筑钦安殿是举行道教活动的场所。钦安殿东南、东北、西南、西北分布万春、浮碧、千秋、澄瑞四亭，代表一年四季。花园西侧有“凹”字形建筑养性斋，与东侧“凸”字形建筑绛雪轩呼应，二者皆曾用作皇帝藏书、读书之所，在花园总体对称的布局中，又显变化活泼的一面。

除建筑外，花园有古树一百余棵，另有奇石造景点缀其间。园内东北角，为形态各异的石头堆砌而成的堆秀山，可供帝后嫔妃登高望远。园中还有“海参石”“木变石”和“诸葛拜斗石”，皆天然形成，相映成趣。

御花园作为紫禁城的重要组成部分，是宫廷政务、生活之余放松身心、陶冶性情的好去处，体现了中国人寄情山水、寓于自然的理想追求。

The Imperial Garden (*Yuhuayuan*)

Located on the northernmost end of the central axis of the Forbidden City, the Imperial Garden covers an area of 12,000 square meters and is the largest garden in the Forbidden City. It served as a recreational and entertainment venue for emperors, empresses, and concubines of the Ming and Qing dynasties.

The garden is dotted with multiple buildings. The main building, the Hall of Imperial Peace, once served as a venue for Taoist activities.

To the southeast, northeast, southwest, and northwest of the Hall of Imperial Peace stand four pavilions that represent the four seasons—the Pavilion of Myriad Springs (*Wanchun ting*), the Pavilion of Floating Jade *(Fubi ting*), the Pavilion of One Thousand Autumns (*Qianqiu ting*), and the Pavilion of Auspicious Lucidity (*Chengrui ting*).

On the western side of the garden is a concave-shaped building called the Lodge of Spiritual Cultivation (*Yangxing zhai*), which symmetrizes the convex-shaped building named the Bower of Crimson Snow (*Jiangxue xuan*) on the eastern side. Both were used by the emperor as venues for book collection and reading. They add a sense of dynamics and liveliness to the overall symmetrical layout of the garden.

More than 100 ancient trees and artificial rockeries dot the garden in addition to the buildings.

In the northeastern corner of the garden stands the Hill of Accumulated Excellence (*Duixiu shan*), built of stones of various shapes, where emperors and imperial consorts could enjoy views from atop the hill.

Another feature is grotesque natural rocks such as the Sea Cucumber Rock, the Wood-turned Stone, and the "Zhuge Liang Worshipping the Big Dipper" Rock, which set off each other.

An important part of the Forbidden City, the Imperial Garden was an ideal place for the emperor to handle state affairs, relax, and seek inner peace, reflecting the Chinese pursuit of finding spiritual resonance in natural landscapes.

角楼

紫禁城城墙的四个拐角，各矗立着一座精美绝伦的角楼。它们坐落于城墙上，优雅身姿倒映于护城河的波光之中，是紫禁城极具标志性的景观之一。

角楼明清多次修缮。主体为亭式建筑，整体轮廓和谐，层次丰富。屋顶为三重檐，由纵横相交的歇山顶构成，上覆黄琉璃瓦，顶部中间置铜鎏金宝顶。角楼的建筑结构复杂而精妙，由多种脊、梁、柱构成，实则仅翼角用梁就多达 56 根。其建造过程更是灵活使用了多种木结构工艺，为中国古代营造技艺之大成。

紫禁城西北角楼东南侧面

The northwest corner tower of the Forbidden City, viewed from the southeast.

Corner Towers (*Jiao Lou*)

At each of the four corners of the Forbidden City is an exquisite corner tower. Standing atop the city wall, the towers, along with their reflections in the moat, have become one of the iconic images of the Forbidden City.

The corner towers were renovated several times during the Ming and Qing dynasties.

The main body is a pavilion-style building, with a harmonious, multi-layered outline. They feature vertical and horizontal intersecting hip-and-gable roofs with triple eaves, covered with yellow glazed tiles and culminating in a gilt copper pinnacle.

Their architectural structure is complex and exquisite, composed of a variety of roof ridges, beams, and columns. Each employs as many as 56 corner beams alone. In the construction process, a variety of wood structure techniques were flexibly used, making them masterpieces in ancient Chinese architecture.

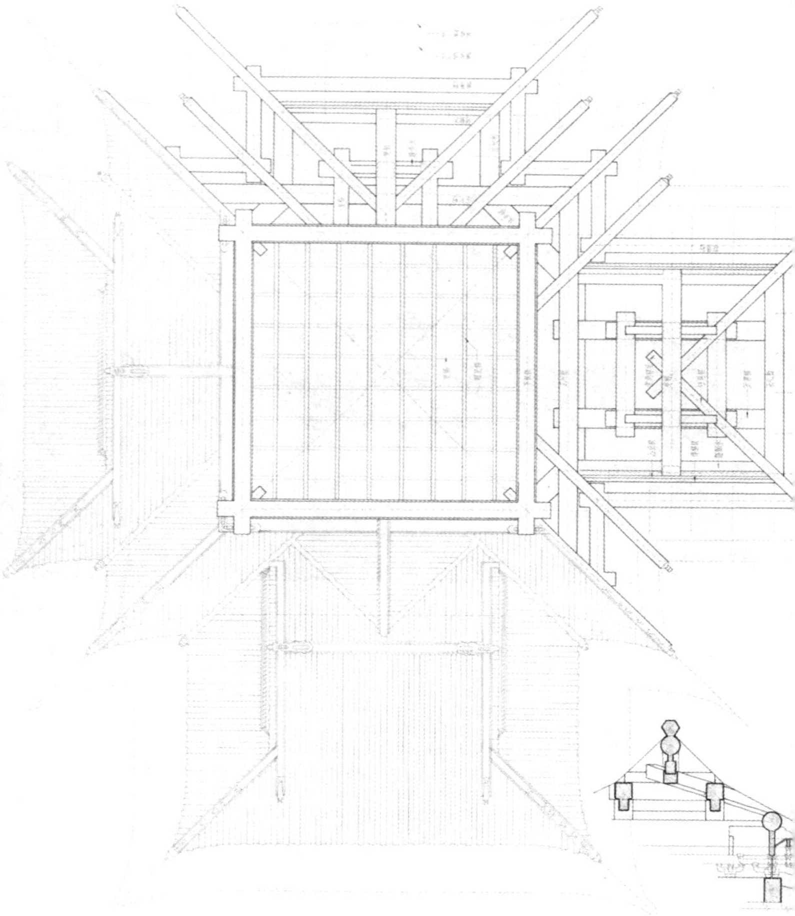

角楼作为瞭望警戒的城防设施，与城垣、城门楼和护城河共同构成紫禁城防御体系，守卫紫禁城数百年。它们继承了我国古代木构建筑灵活多变的传统作法，使用功能和装饰效果得以巧妙地结合，展现出我国古代匠师们的高超技艺和卓越才能。

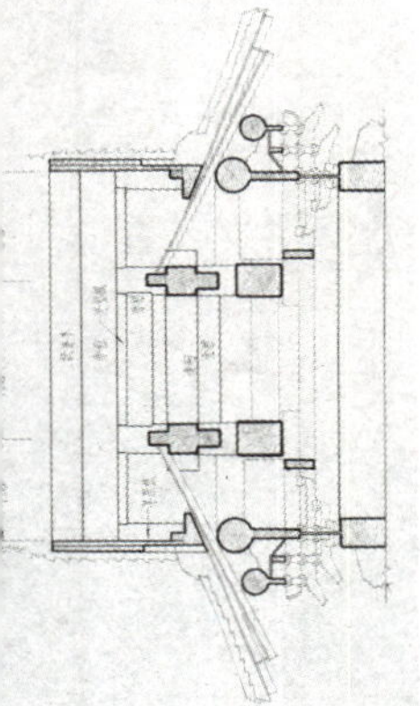

紫禁城角楼第三层平面图，可见角楼内部复杂的梁柱结构

A plan drawing of the third floor of a corner tower of the Forbidden City showcases the intricate pillar and beam structures inside.

As watchtowers for defense purposes, the corner towers, alongside the city wall, gate towers, and moat, formed the defense system of the Forbidden City, guarding the former imperial palace for hundreds of years.

They inherited flexible and varied traditional techniques for wooden buildings in China, and perfectly combined functions and decorative effects, demonstrating superb skills and outstanding talent of ancient Chinese craftsmen.

三

上古至元文化遗珍

故宫博物院的文物藏品，如同一部鲜活的历史长卷，从新石器时代的质朴玉石器，到被誉为“天下第一行书”的《兰亭序》、天才画家传世名作《千里江山图》、享誉世界的元代青花釉里红，每一件文物都是“国宝”。这些藏品不仅连缀成一部不间断的物质文明史，更向世界生动展现了中华民族持续不断、灿烂多彩的物质生活与精神世界，是人类文明宝库中的瑰宝。

RELICS FROM THE PREHISTORIC PERIOD TO THE YUAN DYNASTY

The relics held by the Palace Museum compose a vivid scroll of history. National treasures range from primitive jade objects of the Neolithic Age to *The Orchid Pavilion Preface* dubbed the "greatest calligraphic work in running script under heaven", *A Panorama of Rivers and Mountains* by a gifted painter, and the world-famous Blue-and-White Porcelain with Under-glazed Red Decorations of the Yuan Dynasty (1206-1368), to name a few only.

These artifacts not only track the uninterrupted history of China's civilization, but also vividly show the continuous, splendid, and colorful material life and spiritual world of the Chinese nation. They are treasures of human civilization.

玉龙

玉龙是一件传世文物，用整块黄绿色闪石玉雕琢而成，像英文字母“C”的形状，首尾相顾、弯曲如虹、遒劲有力。龙头雕琢简洁流畅，嘴部用寥寥数笔阴刻线条勾勒出颚部轮廓，鼻上翘，双目凸起，硬朗有神。颈背长鬃飘逸，潇洒灵动。龙身光素无纹，无角无鳞，中部有孔，两面对穿，若以绳系孔悬置，则玉龙水平平衡。

它来自著名古玉研究专家、收藏家傅忠谟先生。该玉龙属于新石器时代红山文化，距今约 6500—5000 年。红山文化因 1935 年在内蒙古赤峰红山发掘而得名，主要分布于东北地区西南部。红山文化出土大量玉器，造型多、技艺巧，有大量动物形象，如鸟、龟等，尤以玉龙最为出名，古朴写意，突显北方民族质朴与豪放的风格。

C 形玉龙是中国出土文物中最早的龙的形象，被称为“中华第一龙”。故宫博物院藏玉龙，长达 60 厘米，在同类藏品中体量最大。

Jade Dragon

A precious relic handed down from generation to generation, the jade dragon was carved from a whole piece of yellow-green nephrite and resembles the letter "C". With its head and tail facing each other, it forms a curve like a rainbow and looks powerful.

The concisely carved dragon head boasts fluent lines, and the mouth and jaw outlines were engraved simply. The nose is upturned, and the eyes are protruding, which look vigorous and spirited. The long mane on the back of the neck is lifelike, as if it were floating.

The dragon is hornless, and its body has no scales or decorative patterns. There is a hole in the middle of its body. If hung by a rope through the hole, the dragon maintains a horizontally balanced position.

The jade dragon was donated by Fu Zhongmo, a renowned ancient jade ware researcher and collector. It comes from the Hongshan Culture of the Neolithic Age, some 5,000-6,500 years ago. The Hongshan Culture was so named because it was discovered in 1935 at the Hongshan Site in Chifeng, Inner Mongolia.

The relics of the Hongshan Culture are mainly scattered in the southwestern quadrant of northeast China. Many jade artifacts from here have been unearthed, featuring a variety of shapes and exquisite techniques. Many are shaped like animals such as birds and tortoises.

The most noticeable are those in the shape of the dragon, which boast primitive beauty and freehand carving and demonstrate the simple and bold artistic style of ethnic groups from north China.

The C-shaped jade dragon is the oldest artifact in the shape of a dragon ever brought to light in China. Now held in the Palace Museum, it is 60 centimeters long, the largest among all artifacts of the same type.

玉龙头部细节

The head of the jade dragon.

莲鹤方壶

莲鹤方壶是春秋时期重器，高122厘米，宽54厘米，重64千克，形体巨大，是用来盛酒的容器。1923年出土于河南新郑，共两件，分别藏于故宫博物院、河南博物院。

方壶由壶盖、壶身组成，运用圆雕、浅浮雕、细刻等多种装饰手法。壶盖装饰双层镂雕莲瓣，中心为灵动欲飞的仙鹤。壶身装饰各种不同形式的龙，腹部饰蟠龙，四角铸飞龙，双耳也为龙。底部由两只卷尾兽承托，稳健有力。

春秋时期，中国青铜器铸造创新"失蜡法"，发扬"分铸法"。"失蜡法"，即以蜡制范配合泥质内、外范制器，高温下蜡熔化流出，浇筑铜液器物成型，可以制作出泥模无法铸造的复杂、精细的器件。"分铸法"则是分别铸造器物各部分，再铸接起来的制作工艺。莲鹤方壶的耳、足和盖上的立鹤即分铸而成，再与壶身铸接于一体。

莲鹤方壶设计奇巧、技艺卓绝，其优美、灵动的造型，与商周青铜器的庄重厚实形成鲜明对比，代表了春秋时期青铜艺术的崭新风格。

Lotus-Crane Square Pot

The Lotus-crane Square Pot is an important artifact from the Spring and Autumn Period (770-476 B.C.). It is a giant wine vessel measuring 122 centimeters in height, 54 centimeters in width, and 64 kilograms in weight. Two pieces were unearthed in 1923 in Xinzheng, today's Henan Province, which are housed in the Palace Museum and Henan Museum, respectively.

The square pot consists of a lid and body and involves a variety of decorative methods such as relief, round sculpture, and fine sculpture. The cover is embellished with two-tiered lotus petals, with a lifelike crane in the center.

The vessel is decorated with dragons of various forms. The belly is adorned with dragon patterns, and each of the four corners has an attached flying dragon. A dragon-shaped handle adorns each side, and dragon patterns fully cover the belly. The vessel is supported by two powerful beasts with curling tails at the bottom.

During the Spring and Autumn Period, Chinese bronze casting innovated the "lost-wax method", and the "separated casting method" became popular.

The lost-wax method is a process using wax and clay molds to cast bronze wares. At high temperatures, the wax is melted and drained away, and then molten metal is injected into the hollowed mold, thus producing complex and exquisite wares that cannot be cast with clay molds alone.

The separated casting method refers to a process in which different parts of an artifact are cast separately and then pieced together. The ears and feet of the lotus-crane square pot and the standing crane on the lid were cast separately and then attached to the body.

The Lotus-crane Square Pot features skillful design, exquisite craftsmanship, and an elegant, vivid shape, which sharply contrast the solemn and sedate style of bronze wares of the Shang (c. 1600-1046 B.C.) and Zhou (1046-256 B.C.) dynasties. It represents the new style of bronze art of the Spring and Autumn Period.

石鼓（吾车刻石）

A stone drum (carved with the poem *Wuche*, meaning “My Chariot”).

石鼓

石鼓为花岗岩材质，因外形似鼓得名，共有十块，表面刻有文字，被称为石鼓文。石鼓文凿刻于春秋战国时期，记录了秦国国君的一场大规模游猎，是中国现存最早的一组石刻文字。

石鼓经历坎坷。它们被发现于唐代，因石鼓文的价值被称颂。唐末战乱，石鼓散失，直到宋代才找回九个。最后一个石鼓被发现时，已流落民间 200 多年，被削去一半，挖成石臼，用于舂米。热爱书法的宋徽宗将全部石鼓运回皇宫，并为铭文填注黄金。金军破宋，石鼓被运往燕京，剔除黄金后再度遗失，重新现世已是元代。此后，石鼓一直被珍藏在北京。1933 年，为避战火，石鼓随故宫文物南迁至四川省，途中遭遇两次翻车仍得以幸存。新中国成立后，石鼓回归故宫博物院。

Stone Drums

The stone drums, made of granite, are so named due to their shape. Ten of such stone drums have been unearthed so far. The writing on them is called stone-drum script.

Known as the earliest stone inscriptions surviving in China, they describe a large-scale hunting expedition by the king of the Qin state in the Spring and Autumn-Warring States Period (770-221 B.C.).

The stone drums endured a turbulent history. They were discovered in the Tang Dynasty (618-907) and already valued for the inscriptions they carry. They were lost in wars at the end of the Tang Dynasty, and nine were recovered until the Song Dynasty (960-1279). By the time the last one was retrieved more than 200 years later, it was cut in half and had been used as a stone mortar to husk rice.

Emperor Huizong of the Song Dynasty, who was obsessed with calligraphy, collected all the stone drums and filled the inscriptions with molten gold.

After the Jin army captured the Song capital, the stone drums were transported to Yanjing (present-day Beijing), where they were lost again after the gold was removed. And they reappeared in the Yuan Dynasty.

From then on, the stone drums had been stored in Beijing. In 1933, they were evacuated southward to Sichuan Province alongside other relics in the collection of the Palace Museum to escape warfare. On the way, the truck transporting the stone drums rolled over twice, but fortunately, they survived. After the founding of the People's Republic of China, the stone drums ultimately returned to the Palace Museum.

被削去一半的乍原刻石

A halved stone drum.

石鼓文为秦大篆，上承商周时期铸于青铜器上的金文字体，下为秦始皇用来统一中国文字的秦小篆奠定基础。石鼓在历史学、文字学、文学和书法领域都具有不可替代的重要价值。

吾水刻石上的石鼓文

Inscriptions on the stone drum carved with the poem *Wushui*, or *My River*.

The inscriptions on the stone drums are the large seal script. This script inherited the bronze inscriptions of the Shang and Zhou dynasties and laid the foundation for the small seal script used by Qin Shi Huang, the first emperor of the Qin Dynasty (221-206 B.C.), to unify the country's writing system. The stone drums are of irreplaceable importance in the fields of history, philology, literature, and calligraphy.

临袁侯铜虎符

临袁侯铜虎符，为西汉早期制品，体量小巧，成年人一手可握。虎呈俯卧状，昂首向前，虎尾向上卷起，侧面有方形凹槽，用于对合时验证真伪。

虎符是将完整的虎形对半分开，一半在君王手中，一半作为军权凭证授予将领，如需调兵，要两半合一。虎符最早出现于春秋时期，盛行于战国秦汉，多用青铜铸成，再刻上文字。

早期的虎符只有一半也可读出信息，自汉代起虎符多将文字置于虎的脊背骑缝处，合符才能读出全部内容，保密性更强。由这件虎符背上的九个错银半字，可知此虎符为左半部分，在统军的临袁侯手中。如需调动军队，君王须派使臣持右半虎符前往临袁侯驻地，合符无误即可发兵。

Bronze Tiger Tally of Marquis Lin Yuan

The Bronze Tiger Tally of Marquis Lin Yuan is an artifact dating back to the early Western Han Dynasty (206 B.C.-A.D. 25). It is so tiny that an adult can hold it in one hand. The tally is in the shape of a lying tiger, with its head protruding forward and its tail rolling upwards. Square grooves on the sides verify authenticity by interlocking.

A tiger tally consists of two halves, with one half held by the monarch and the other by the commanding officer as a symbol of military authority. The officer would only accept orders accompanied by interlocking the other half.

Tiger tallies originated in the Spring and Autumn Period and were most commonly used in the Warring States Period and Qin and Han dynasties. Most were cast in bronze and engraved with inscriptions.

One can read information from the inscriptions on only one half of an early tiger tally. From the Han Dynasty (206 B.C.-A.D. 220), inscriptions were usually carved on the tiger's back separated into two halves, and the message they carry can be legible only when the two halves are pieced together, thus enhancing the confidentiality.

With nine incomplete characters on the tiger's back, this is the left half of a tiger tally owned by Marquis Lin Yuan who commanded the army. To move the troops, the emperor needed to send an envoy with the right half to the garrison of Marquis Lin Yuan, who would accept the order when the two halves matched.

虎符脊背处的铭文
Inscriptions on the back of the tiger tally.

虎符独特的设计和工艺是研究中国古代兵权制度和军事管理方式的珍贵资料，同时也是中国古代早期军事保密方法的实证，其配对验证思路与现代保密技术有异曲同工之处。

The unique design and craftsmanship of the tiger tally provides valuable references to the study of the military authority system and army management methods in ancient China. It is also the physical evidence of early encryption methods in the military of ancient China, and its authenticity verifying approach is similar to modern encryption techniques.

彩绘漆鸟纹耳杯

彩绘漆鸟纹耳杯是一件西汉时期的漆制酒杯，出土于湖北省荆州市的西汉墓。它杯口椭圆，浅腹弧壁，两侧杯耳呈新月形，耳面上翘。杯为木胎，漆色外黑内红。内底正中绘有一只翘起长尾的小鸟，鸟的轮廓、足、尾由黑线勾勒，鸟身与翅膀为黄绿色。杯耳正面及侧面用红漆绘有涡纹。

早在 8000 年前，中国先民就已将漆作为涂料应用。汉代，青铜器逐渐衰落，瓷器还未广受推崇，漆器步入鼎盛时期，制作工艺与艺术水平都获得极大提升。从大量汉代出土文物来看，漆器被广泛应用于生活。

Painted Lacquer Ear Cup with Bird Pattern

The Painted Lacquer Ear Cup with Bird Pattern, unearthed from a tomb in Jingzhou City, Hubei Province, is a lacquered wine vessel dating back to the Western Han Dynasty.

It features an oval mouth, a shallow belly with an arced wall, and two crescent-shaped ears upturned on both sides. Made of wood, the cup is painted black on the outside and red inside. At the center of the inside bottom is a small bird with a long tail, whose body, feet, and tail were drawn with black lines. Its body and wings are yellow-green. There are red-lacquered swirl patterns on the front and sides of the cup's ears.

As early as 8,000 years ago, Chinese ancestors used lacquer as a coating material.

In the Han Dynasty, when bronzeware gradually declined and porcelain had yet to gain popularity, lacquerware welcomed its heyday as both production techniques and artistic representation reached full maturity.

Based on the large quantity of unearthed relics from the Han Dynasty, researchers agree that lacquerware was widely used in everyday life at that time.

耳杯内底的鸟纹

A bird pattern on the inside bottom of the ear cup.

耳杯又称“羽觞”，出现于春秋战国时期，是中国传统的饮酒器具。因器薄轻便，耳杯还被盛酒后放入流水，作为古代文人饮酒赋诗的一种游戏器具。

此耳杯造型简洁流畅，图案生动写实，笔触精细，显现出西汉漆器装饰纹样的典型特征，是实用与美观结合的典范。

As traditional wine vessels in ancient China, ear cups, also known as *yushang* (drinking vessels), originated in the Spring and Autumn-Warring States Period.

Given that they are thin and light, ear cups with wine were floated down a running stream, a game popular among ancient literati when they drank while composing poems.

This ear cup features a simple and streamlined shape as well as vivid and exquisite decorative patterns, demonstrating the typical style of the decorative patterns of Western Han lacquerware. It is considered an exemplary artifact integrating aesthetics with practicality.

青釉堆塑谷仓罐

青釉堆塑谷仓罐是三国时期江南吴地的陪葬品，距今已1700余年。

器物通体施青釉，主体为一大罐，上面堆有5只相连的小罐，中心罐口还探出一只口叼食物的小老鼠。小罐四周堆塑出多种装饰，居中者为三层楼阁，阁前有两只小狗看门。两侧门阙旁，八位侍仆正卖力演奏乐器，周围鸟雀则引颈觅食，呈现出欢庆丰收、百鸟争食的热闹场景。在罐子肩部，塑贴了一只小乌龟，背驮“石碑”，上刻24字，寄托吉祥寓意的同时，也点明了器物制作的时间：东吴永安三年（260）。龟四周贴塑鹿、猪、鱼等动物。

这件精美的陪葬器物表现了当时富裕人家的日常生活情景，也反映出中国人“事死如事生”的生命哲理观。

青釉堆塑谷仓罐局部

Part of the Green-Glazed Barn-Shaped Jar with Modeled Decorations.

Green-Glazed Barn-Shaped Jar with Modeled Decorations

The Green-Glazed Barn-Shaped Jar with Modeled Decorations is a burial object dating back to the Three Kingdoms Period (220-280) in the Wu region of south China, with a history of more than 1,700 years.

The artifact is entirely coated by green glaze and consists of a big jar and five interconnected smaller jars on the top. A small mouse holding food in its mouth peeks out from the mouth of the big jar.

Around the smaller jars are modeled decorations. In the middle is a three-story pavilion, in front of which stands two puppies guarding the gate. Eight attendants are playing musical instruments beside the two gate towers on both sides while birds look for food. Together, it is a joyful scene depicting a harvest celebration.

A tiny tortoise is affixed to the shoulder of the jar. It carries a “stone stele” with 24 Chinese characters, which convey a prayer for good luck and indicate that the burial object was produced in 260 of the Kingdom of Wu (222-280). Surrounding the tortoise are animals such as deer, pigs, and fish.

This exquisite burial object not only depicts the daily life of wealthy families at that time, but also reflects the Chinese afterlife belief that the souls of the dead live in another world.

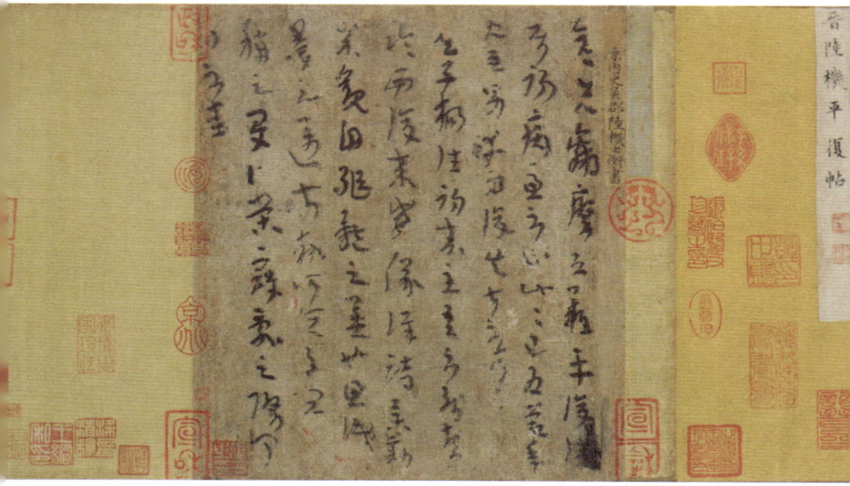

陆机《平复帖》

《平复帖》是西晋文学家、书法家陆机唯一存世的书法作品，以草隶书写于牙色麻纸上，共 9 行 86 字，是陆机写给友人问候疾病的信札，用笔质朴古雅。因写到病体“恐难平复”，故名《平复帖》。

此帖先后被历代多名官员和文人收藏。清朝灭亡后，归末代皇帝溥仪堂兄、书画家溥儒所有。当时皇室后人多靠变卖收藏维持生计，收藏家张伯驹恐国宝流失海外，先后三次向溥儒提出购买。1937 年，溥儒因为母治丧急需款项，张伯驹以四万元重金购得此帖。1956 年，张伯驹夫妇将《平复帖》等多幅书法和绘画名迹捐赠国家，该帖最终由故宫博物院收藏。

《平复帖》是现存最早且流传有序的名家书法真迹，有“法帖之祖”的美誉，对书法风格演变和西晋文化研究有着极为重要的意义。

A Consoling Letter (*Pingfu Tie*) by Lu Ji

A Consoling Letter is the only existing calligraphic work by Lu Ji, a renowned writer and calligrapher in the Western Jin Dynasty (265-317). With 86 Chinese characters inscribed on a piece of linen paper in nine lines, it is a letter written by Lu to console his sick friend, hence its name.

Historically, this calligraphic work had been successively held by several officials and scholars of different periods.

After the collapse of the Qing Dynasty, it was acquired by calligrapher and painter Pu Ru, who was a cousin of Puyi, the last emperor of China. Back then, many descendants of the Qing royal family made a living selling their collections.

Chinese collector Zhang Boju feared that this national treasure would be lost overseas, so he proposed to Pu Ru three times to buy the calligraphic work. In 1937, Pu Ru was in urgent need of money for his mother's funeral and sold it to Zhang at a price of 40,000 yuan. In 1956, Zhang Boju and his wife donated several calligraphy and painting masterpieces, including *A Consoling Letter*, to the government, which is now held in the Palace Museum.

A Consoling Letter is the oldest authentic work by a famous ancient calligrapher that has been handed down to this day. Dubbed the "Ancestor of Model Calligraphy", it is of great importance to study the evolution of calligraphic styles and the Western Jin culture.

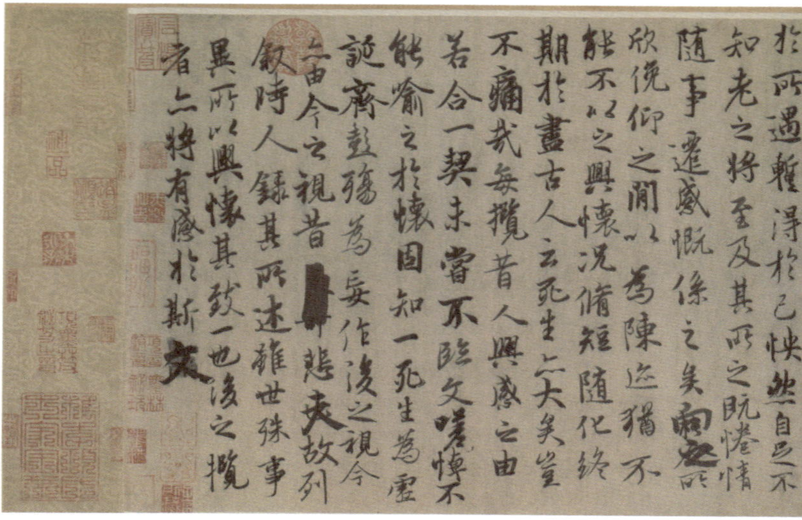

神龙本《兰亭序》

《兰亭序》是东晋书法家王羲之的名作，被誉为“天下第一行书”。原作已不知所终，有众多复本传世。其中最著名的神龙本《兰亭序》，相传为唐代拓书人冯承素勾摹。因画心首尾分别有唐中宗李显的神龙年号半印，故称“神龙本”。

东晋文人流行雅集活动。永和九年（353），王羲之与多位友人在兰亭行修禊（xì）之礼（中国古代的一种风俗，到水边洗濯嬉游，并举行祈福消灾的仪式），沐浴春风，去除晦气和不祥。他们围坐在流水边，将盛满酒的羽觞顺水漂下，羽觞受阻停在谁面前，谁就要饮酒作诗，此即曲水流觞。诗汇成诗集，由王羲之

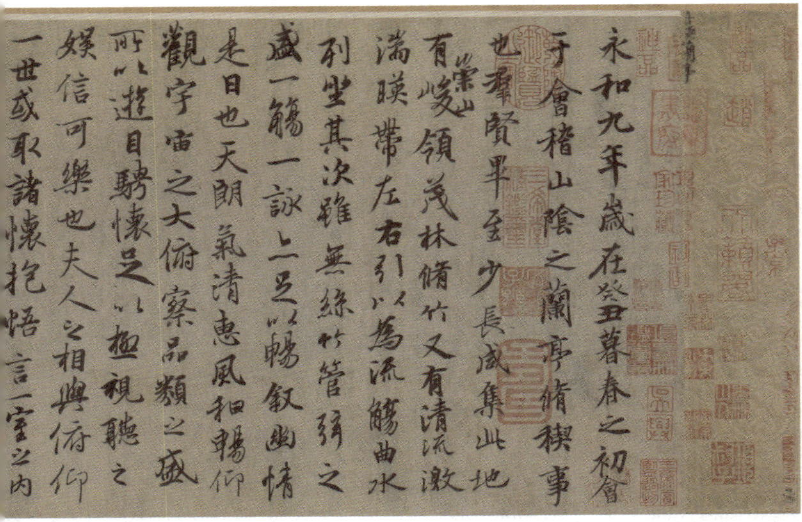

The Orchid Pavilion Preface with the Mark of Shenlong

Acclaimed as the "greatest work in running script under heaven", *The Orchid Pavilion Preface* is a masterpiece by Wang Xizhi, a renowned calligrapher in the Eastern Jin Dynasty (317-420).

The original work has been lost, but many duplicates have been preserved to this day, of which the most famous is *The Orchid Pavilion Preface* with the mark of Shenlong.

Most agree that this piece was a copy by Feng Chengsu, a rubbing expert in the Tang Dynasty. The calligraphic work was so named because it carries the halved seal of Shenlong, the reign title of Li Xian, or Emperor Zhongzong of the Tang Dynasty.

The literati in the Eastern Jin Dynasty often held meetings known as *yaji* (elegant gatherings).

In 353, Wang Xizhi and a group of his friends performed *xiuxi* (a ritual to pray for blessings and ward off disasters by bathing and playing in rivers in ancient China) at the Orchid Pavilion. There, they basked in the spring breeze in hopes of escaping misfortune.

They sat by a running stream and floated a wine cup on it.

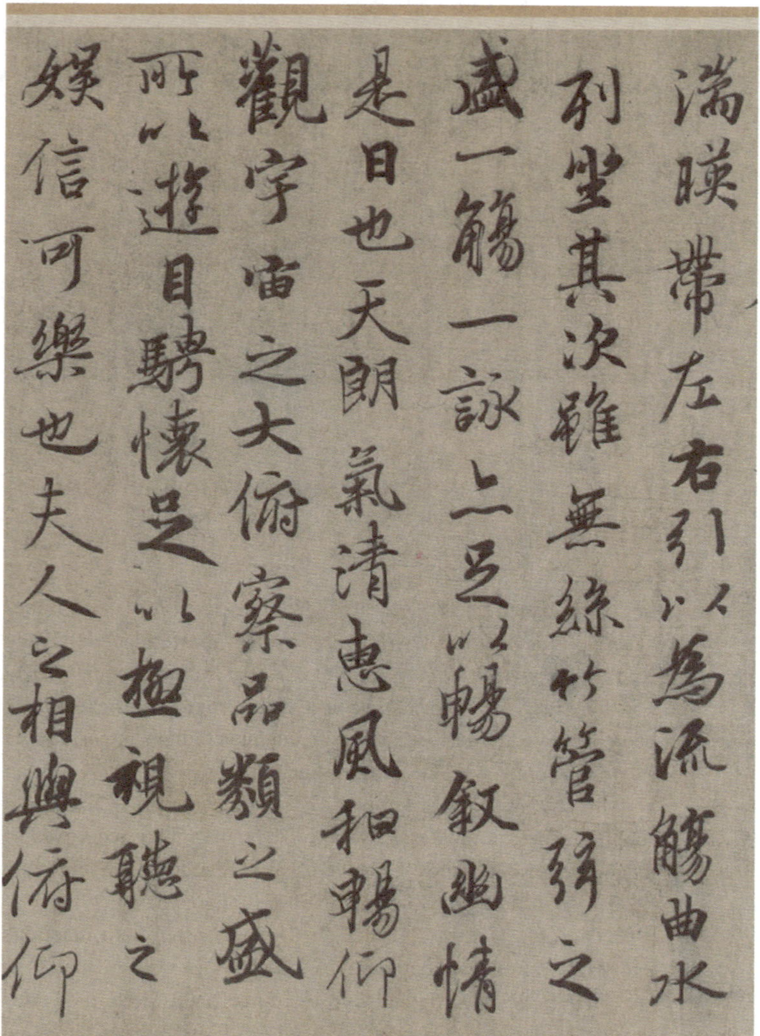

神龙本《兰亭序》局部

Part of *The Orchid Pavilion Preface* with the Mark of Shenlong.

现场作序，记录当时盛况并抒发内心感慨。曲水流觞也因此逐渐成为一种文人雅事。

神龙本《兰亭序》摹写精美，字的笔画结构自然生动，既保留了原作的改写痕迹，又像自由书写一般充满神韵，具有极高的艺术价值。

When the cup stopped before a person, he had to drink the wine and compose a poem. This practice was known as "drifting cups on a meandering stream".

The poems they composed were later made into a collection, with Wang Xizhi writing a preface for it to describe the scene of the gathering and express his feelings. From then on, "drifting cups on a meandering stream" gradually became an elegant pastime popular among the literati.

The Orchid Pavilion Preface with the mark of Shenlong is an exquisite copy featuring fluent and dynamic strokes, which not only maintains the changes on the original work, but also displays the charm of free writing and high artistic value.

“大圣遗音”琴

古琴又称七弦琴，是中国传统乐器之一。现存传世最早的古琴流传自唐代。

“大圣遗音”琴是中唐时期古琴。桐木做成，琴面如弓，栗壳色漆，间有黑色，局部略有朱漆修补。背面圆孔和扁长圆孔，用于散音，叫作龙池、凤沼。此面还刻有草书“大圣遗音”，以及铭文“巨壑迎秋，寒江印月。万籁悠悠，孤桐飒裂”。

"*Da Sheng Yi Yin*" Guqin

The *guqin*, also called the seven-stringed zither, is a traditional Chinese musical instrument. The oldest *guqin* existing today can be traced back to the Tang Dynasty.

This one, dating back to the mid-Tang Dynasty, derived its name from four Chinese characters "大圣遗音" in cursive script on its body, pronounced as "*Da Sheng Yi Yin*", literally meaning "Musical Legacy of the Sage".

The surface of the *guqin*, made of paulownia wood, resembles a bow, painted with chestnut-colored lacquer, with black in between. Some parts were slightly repaired with vermilion lacquer.

The round hole and the oblong hole on the back were designed for sound diffusion, which are called *longchi* (dragon's pond) and *fengzhao* (phoenix's pool), respectively. The *guqin* also carries inscriptions that translate to "As the autumn wind blows in the giant gully and the moon is reflected on the cold river, the melodic sound

“大圣遗音”琴背面铭文

此琴原藏于皇帝的珍品库养心殿南库。溥仪出宫后，清室善后委员会发现因南库年久失修漏雨，琴面上凝结了一层水锈，琴色灰白，破败不堪。直至 1947 年，故宫博物院邀请著名古琴家管平湖前来修理数月后，“大圣遗音”琴才恢复原有神采。管平湖将琴修好后曾试弹，琴音清脆松透，音质极佳。

古人认为最好的琴音具有九德，即奇、古、透、润、静、圆、匀、清、芳九个特点，给人完美悦耳的听觉享受。具备“九德”的琴少有，但“大圣遗音”琴“九德”兼具，是传世古琴中的至品。

of the *guqin* breaks the silence".

This musical instrument was formerly stored in the southern warehouse in the Hall of Mental Cultivation, where the emperor stored his treasures.

After the last emperor Puyi moved out of the Forbidden City, the committee responsible for handling the aftermath of the Qing court discovered that after years of neglect, the roof of the southern warehouse was leaking on rainy days. For this reason, a layer of scale condensed on the surface of the *guqin*, making it dilapidated and almost unfunctional.

In 1947, the Palace Museum invited famous *guqin* expert Guan Pinghu to repair it. After months of efforts, the instrument was restored. When Guan tried it after the repair, the *guqin* produced a clear and melodious sound.

The ancient Chinese believed that an excellent *guqin* had "nine virtues"—being unique, ancient, clear, smooth, tranquil, harmonious, balanced, pure, and fragrant. These qualities together provide a perfect, pleasing auditory experience. However, few had all nine virtues. The "*Da Sheng Yi Yin*" *guqin* stands out among its counterparts for owning all of them.

《五牛图》

《五牛图》是唐代政治家、画家韩滉（723—787）的传世画作，黄麻纸本设色手卷，是现存最早的纸本绘画。

画面描绘了五头神态各异的牛，一络首而立、一回首舐舌、一昂头行走、一俯身蹭痒，中间一牛最为特别，正对观画者，准确表现透视关系。五头牛神采奕奕，动态十足。厚重多变的线条、浓淡晕染的色彩、对于眼睛和毛皮的细节刻画，均体现出作者高超的造型能力。

该卷经南宋内府、清代内府及名家赵孟頫、项元汴等收藏，清末因战争被掠走。1950 年，周恩来总理收到爱国人士来信，得知《五牛图》即将在香港出售的消息，立即下达指示，要求不

《五牛图》局部

Part of the handscroll *Five Oxen* by Han Huang.

Five Oxen

Five Oxen is a color handscroll drawn by Tang-dynasty politician and painter Han Huang (723-787) on a piece of yellow linen paper. It is the oldest paper painting surviving to this day.

The painting depicts five oxen with different postures: One stands with its heads up, another sticks out its tongue while looking back, one walks with its head held high, another leans down to scratch against a rock, and the one in the middle is the most special—it seems to be gazing at the viewer.

The entire painting displays an accurate perspective. The five oxen radiate with vitality and dynamics. The thick and varied lines, the shades of color, and the detailed depiction of the eyes and fur all reflect the painter's superb skills.

The scroll painting was successively collected by the royal courts of the Southern Song Dynasty (1127-1279) and the Qing Dynasty as well as by such famous painters and collectors as Zhao Mengfu and Xiang Yuanbian. It was plundered in wartime at the end of the Qing Dynasty.

In 1950, then Premier Zhou Enlai received a letter from a patriot who revealed that *Five Oxen* was about to be auctioned in Hong Kong. Zhou immediately ordered action to prevent the national treasure from being lost again at all costs.

After expert appraisal and several rounds of negotiations, the painting was brought back to Beijing at a price of HK$60,000. By that time, however, the painting had been severely damaged. It was

惜一切代价阻止国宝流失。经专家鉴定和多次交涉，最终以 6 万港币购回祖国，但此时的《五牛图》已残破不堪，经过故宫专家精心修复与重裱，终于恢复了完整面目。

《五牛图》代表了中晚唐时期以牛为主题绘画的巅峰水平，被列为“中国十大传世名画”之一。观众得以透过《五牛图》了解宰相韩滉对“民生多艰”的关注，学习牛身上具备的朴实无华、善良忠诚的宝贵精神。

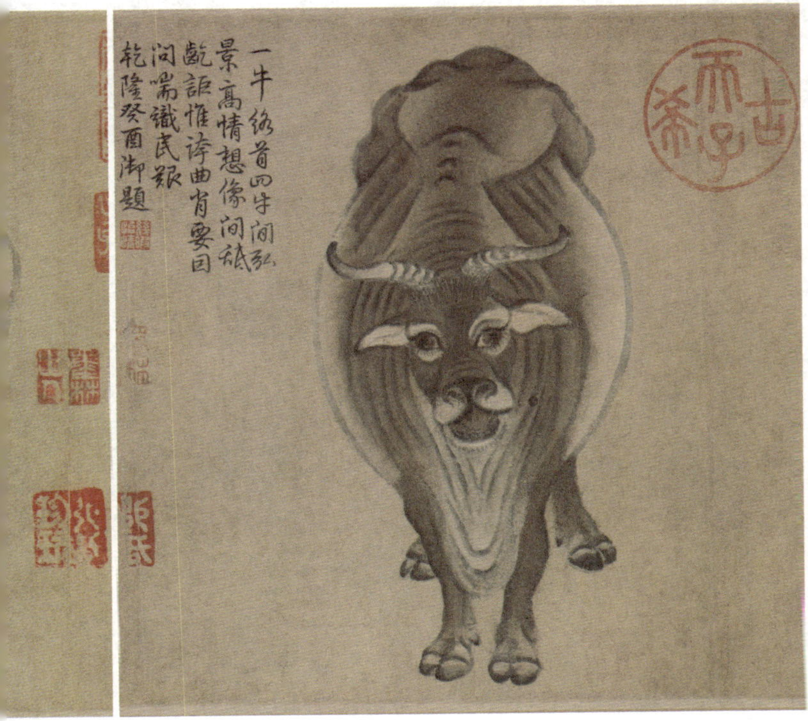

《五牛图》局部

Part of the handscroll *Five Oxen* by Han Huang.

finally restored thanks to the careful repairing and remounting by experts from the Palace Museum.

Five Oxen represents the pinnacle of ox-themed painting in the mid- and late Tang Dynasty and has been listed as one of the "Top Ten Famous Paintings of All Ages in China". Through the painting, viewers can sense a hint of sympathy that the painter, who was a prime minister, held for the hardships of the common people, while admiring the virtues of simplicity, kindness, and loyalty often associated with oxen.

《清明上河图》

《清明上河图》是北宋宫廷画家张择端仅见的传世精品。绢本设色长卷，描绘了北宋都城汴京的繁盛面貌和各阶层人民的生活状态。

全卷分为城郊风景、虹桥两岸的商贸活动、市区街道景观三部分。长达 5 米的画卷里，绘制了各色人物 500 余人，船只 20 余艘，各种车马、房屋、桥梁等鳞次栉比，随处可见。

细看画面，可以看到运货的驼队、忙碌的码头、热闹的各色商铺、宏伟的城门。其中最精彩的一幕是虹桥下一艘货船正

《清明上河图》（局部） 各色商铺

Various types of shops depicted in *Along the River During the Qingming Festival.*

Along the River During the Qingming Festival

Along the River During the Qingming Festival is the only painting masterpiece by Song-dynasty court painter Zhang Zeduan that has been preserved to this day. A long color scroll painting on silk, it depicts the prosperity of Bianliang, capital of the Northern Song Dynasty (960-1127), as well as the lives of people from all walks of life at that time.

The painting consists of three sections which depict suburban landscapes, commercial activities on both sides of the Rainbow Bridge and the views of urban streets, respectively. The 5-meter-long scroll portrays 500-plus figures, more than 20 ships, as well as various vehicles, horses, houses, and bridges.

Upon viewing the painting carefully, one can see camel caravans transporting goods, busy wharves, shops packed with customers, and tall and magnificent city gates.

One of the most eye-catching sights is a cargo ship about

《清明上河图》（局部）　城门和商队

The city gate and merchant caravan depicted in *Along the River During the Qingming Festival.*

待过桥，船夫们有的撑船，有的拉纤绳，有的急忙放下桅杆，以便船只通过。桥上的行人也伸出头来，指挥着，吆喝着。作者将景色、人物刻画得生动逼真，画面布局错落有致。

《清明上河图》不仅仅是一件伟大的现实主义绘画艺术珍品，同时也为我们提供了北宋大都市的商业、手工业、民俗、建筑、交通工具等翔实形象的第一手资料，具有重要历史文献价值。其丰富的思想内涵、独特的审美视角、现实主义的表现手法，都使其在中国乃至世界绘画史上被奉为经典之作。

《清明上河图》（局部）虹桥

The Rainbow Bridge depicted in *Along the River During the Qingming Festival.*

to pass under the Rainbow Bridge, on which some boatmen are punting, some are pulling the towrope, and others are busy lowering the mast so that the ship can pass. Pedestrians on the bridge are sticking out their heads to shout at the sailors. The painter vividly portrayed the scenes and figures, composing a well-designed layout.

A realist painting masterpiece, *Along the River During the Qingming Festival* provides first-hand information on the commerce, handicrafts, folk customs, architecture, and transportation of the capital of the Northern Song Dynasty, giving it high historical value. Its rich cultural connotation, unique aesthetic perspective, and realistic expression techniques have made it a classic in the art history of China and even the world.

《千里江山图》

《千里江山图》是北宋画家王希孟绘制的山水长卷，堪称宋代青绿山水画中的鸿篇巨制。王希孟作画时年仅 18 岁，这也是他唯一传世的作品。

《千里江山图》以石青、石绿等矿物质为主要颜料绘成，用色夸张艳丽，色泽持久。画卷仅画心即近 12 米，大致分为六个部分，每部分以山为主体，用桥和流水衔接过渡。图中所绘山峦，或高耸入云，或绵延起伏，层峦叠翠间，亦可领略江河之烟波浩渺。细看山水之中，有瀑布高挂山崖，有山间茂林修竹，有水边岸芷汀兰，村落、寺庙、亭台水榭、瓦屋茅舍等，隐于其中。渔人农夫忙于生计，书生隐士或群聚社交，或独自赏景，形象虽细小如豆，行态却生动鲜明。

《千里江山图》局部

Part of *A Panorama of Rivers and Mountains*.

A Panorama of Rivers and Mountains

A Panorama of Rivers and Mountains is a landscape scroll by Wang Ximeng, a renowned painter during the Northern Song Dynasty. It is regarded as a masterpiece of Song-dynasty blue-green landscape paintings. Wang completed the painting at the age of 18, and it is his only work to be preserved to present day.

The painting mainly uses pigments made of minerals such as azurite and malachite, and the colors are exaggerated, gorgeous, and long-lasting. Nearly 12 meters long, it is roughly divided into six parts, each with mountains as the mainstay, connected by bridges and flowing rivers. The mountains in the painting are either towering into the clouds or rolling and undulating.

One can appreciate the vastness of forested mountains and meandering rivers. Looking closely, one will see waterfalls hanging high on the cliffs, lush forests and bamboos on the mountains, and blooming flowers on the riverside as well as villages, temples, pavilions, and tiled or thatched houses scattered around. Fishermen and farmers are busy working, and scholars and hermits are either socializing in groups or enjoying the scenery alone. Each figure, though tiny, is vividly portrayed.

《千里江山图》以精炼的手法、绚丽的色彩和细致的描绘，呈现出人们在青山绿水中安居乐业、各得其所的景象，不仅是画家高超技法的反映，更是时代英才胸中的锦绣山河。

《千里江山图》(局部)　画面绘有渔船和村落

The fishing boats and village depicted in *A Panorama of Rivers and Mountains.*

With refined techniques, bright colors, and meticulous depictions, *A Panorama of Rivers and Mountains* presents a scene of people enjoying their lives with contentment in lush mountains and lucid waters. It not only reflects the painter's superb skills, but also presents an ideal world of beauty and harmony in his mind.

汝窑弦纹樽式炉

汝窑弦纹樽式炉，通体施天青色釉，釉面莹润，有细碎开片，并装饰数道弦纹。炉直口，底部为三只蹄形足。造型取自汉代铜器。汉代铜三足樽均与三足承盘配套使用。由此推断，此件器物与故宫所藏汝窑三足承盘搭配使用。

汝窑为北宋五大名窑，窑址位于河南省宝丰县，北宋时归汝州管辖，因而称“汝窑”。汝窑为宫廷烧造青瓷，用工极为讲究，瓷胎香灰色，釉天青色，烧造时多用细小支钉，以使支钉与胎体的接触点尽可能最小。这件汝瓷底部有 5 个支钉痕，俗称芝麻钉痕。

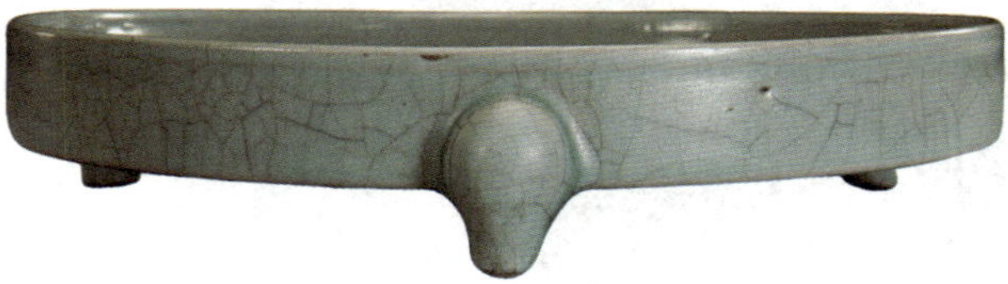

汝窑三足樽承盘

The tripod supporting plate of the *zun*-shaped censor produced by the Ru Kiln.

Zun-Shaped Censer with String Patterns Produced by the Ru Kiln

This *zun*-shaped censer, produced by the Ru Kiln, is coated with lustrous azure glaze and decorated with several string patterns, with tiny cracks. Modeled after the bronze ware of the Han Dynasty, the censer has a straight mouth and three hoof-shaped legs. Since the tripod bronze *zun* (wine vessel) was often used in tandem with a tripod plate in the Han Dynasty, it has been conjectured that this censer was used with the tripod *zun* plate produced by the Ru Kiln, which is also collected in the Palace Museum.

The Ru Kiln, located in Baofeng County, Henan Province, was one of the five most famous kilns in the Northern Song Dynasty. Back then, it was under the jurisdiction of Ru Prefecture, hence its name.

The kiln was responsible for producing celadon ware for the royal court. Its products were admired for their exquisite craftsmanship, distinctive incense ash-colored porcelain bodies, and azure glaze. When fired in the kiln, they were supported by several tiny nails. On the bottom of this censer are five small punctures left by the nails, which are called "sesame nail traces".

汝窑弦纹樽式炉（底部）可见芝麻钉痕

The “sesame nail traces” on the bottom of the *zun*-shaped censer with string patterns produced by the Ru Kiln.

该炉为清宫旧藏。清宫对汝瓷极为珍视，专门定级、配座、指定陈设地点，有的并刻御制诗。与此炉搭配的三足承盘，即刻有乾隆四十三年（1778）御制诗一首。汝瓷作为宋代瓷器之冠，世界范围内藏量极少。已知传世汝窑三足樽式炉仅 3 件，故宫所藏釉质最佳，另两件分别藏于英国大维德基金会、美国辛辛那提艺术博物馆。

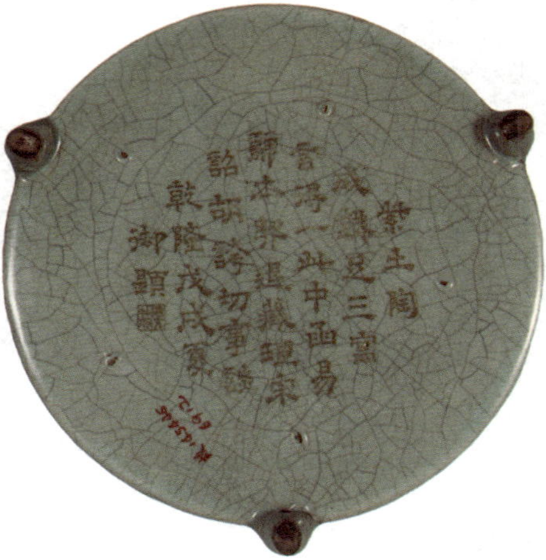

汝窑三足樽承盘（底部）

The bottom of the tripod supporting plate of the *zun*-shaped censer produced by the Ru Kiln.

The censer was once held by the Qing court. The Qing rulers cherished porcelain wares from the Ru Kiln very much, not only rating them and adding supporting stands but also designating a special location to display them, with some engraved with poems by emperors. The tripod plate corresponding to this censer features a poem written by Emperor Qianlong in 1778.

Porcelain wares produced by the Ru Kiln are acclaimed as the "best of the Song-dynasty porcelains", with only a few surviving to this day around the world. So far, only three tripod *zun*-shaped censers from the Ru Kiln have been preserved to this day, of which the one collected in the Palace Museum is best glazed. The other two are held by the Percival David Foundation of Chinese Art in Britain and the Cincinnati Art Museum in the United States, respectively.

白釉孩儿枕

白釉孩儿枕是北宋年间定窑烧制的瓷枕。定窑是中国五大名窑之一，以烧制白瓷闻名。瓷枕最早出现于隋代，盛行于唐、宋、元。古人使用瓷枕，以其能爽身明目、益睛怡神。

这件孩儿枕胎体厚重，通体施白釉，微泛牙黄。孩童俯卧在床榻上，背部作为枕面。他身着素面坎肩、团花纹长袍，双手环抱垫起头部，右手持绣球，双足交叉上翘，天真可爱，生动传神。身下的床榻刻有螭龙垂云纹。造型、纹饰和温润的釉色，均体现出宋代定窑白瓷烧造的高超水平。台北故宫博物院也藏有一件定窑白釉孩儿枕，底部刻有乾隆皇帝警醒自我的御制诗。两件瓷枕造型相近，衣着纹饰明显不同。

这件孩儿枕是中国陶瓷史上的经典之作，是研究宋代文化风俗和陶瓷艺术的珍贵实物。

White-Glazed Boy-Shaped Porcelain Pillow

孩儿枕衣着纹饰（整体图）

An overview of the boy-shaped porcelain pillow.

The white-glazed boy-shaped porcelain pillow was produced by the Ding Kiln in the Northern Song Dynasty. One of the five most famous kilns in ancient China, the Ding Kiln was celebrated for white porcelain.

Porcelain pillows emerged in the Sui Dynasty (581-618), and prevailed in the Tang, Song, and Yuan dynasties. The ancients believed that porcelain pillows could refresh the body and benefit the eyes.

This porcelain pillow features a stout body coated with white glaze and emitting a yellowish ivory luster. It features a lying boy with his back functioning as the pillow surface.

The boy wears a plain vest and a robe embroidered with round flower patterns. He holds an embroidered ball in his right hand, with his arms crossed under his head, and his feet lifting upward. The boy looks innocent, cute, and lifelike. The bed beneath him is engraved with dragon and cloud patterns. The shape, decorative patterns, and lustrous glaze of the pillow all reflect the superb white porcelain firing techniques of the Ding Kiln during the Song Dynasty.

The Palace Museum in Taipei also houses a white-glazed boy-shaped porcelain pillow produced by the Ding Kiln. The bottom of the pillow is engraved with a poem by Emperor Qianlong to exhort himself. The two porcelain pillows are similar in shape, but the clothing patterns are different.

A representative masterpiece in the history of Chinese ceramics, this boy-shaped porcelain pillow is a precious artifact to study the culture, lifestyles, and ceramic art of the Song Dynasty.

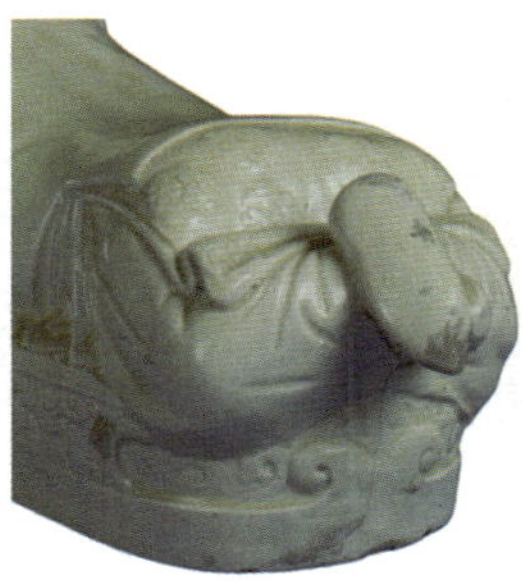

孩儿枕衣着纹饰（局部）

A close-up view of the clothing patterns of the boy-shaped porcelain pillow.

青花釉里红盖罐

青花釉里红镂雕盖罐于1965年出土于河北省保定市元代窖藏，器物造型饱满，通体施青白釉，盖子上的小狮子憨态可掬。罐腹局部镂空，雕饰怪石、牡丹、菊花等。器身蓝、红两种颜色对比强烈，为施在胎体之上、釉面之下的青花和釉里红。二者经一次烧制显出蓝、红色，并不容易实现，这种技艺出现在元代。青花采用钴料呈色，性质稳定，呈色不难。釉里红则采用铜料，呈现红色难度较大，对瓷窑温度和氧气含量等要求极高。因此颜色完美的青花釉里红成器非常难得。

这件器物不仅造型优美、颜色艳丽，还使用了绘画、浮雕、贴塑等多种装饰技法，体现出元代高超的青花釉里红烧造技术。

Lidded Jar with Blue-and-White and Under-Glazed Red Decorations

The Lidded Jar with Blue-and-White and Under-glazed Red Decorations was unearthed in 1965 from a Yuan-dynasty kiln site in Baoding City, north China's Hebei Province. Coated with blue-and-white glaze, the jar has a cute little lion on the lid. The belly is engraved with grotesque rocks, peony, chrysanthemum, and other decorations.

The body features blue and red colors under the glaze, which contrast sharply with each other. It isn't easy to generate both blue and red colors through a single firing process, and this technique didn't emerge until the Yuan Dynasty. The blue color is attributed to pigment made of cobalt, which is stable in nature and easy to achieve. However, the red color under the glaze, which uses pigment made of copper, is difficult to achieve due to extremely high requirements for the temperature and oxygen content of the kiln. Therefore, perfectly colored blue-and-white porcelain objects with under-glazed red decorations are very rare.

This artifact not only has an elegant shape and bright colors but also features a variety of decorative techniques such as painting, hollowed-out carving, and molding, reflecting the superb firing technology for blue-and-white porcelain with under-glazed red decorations in the Yuan Dynasty.

青花釉里红盖罐局部

Part of the Lidded Jar with Blue-and-White and Under-glazed Red Decorations.

朱碧山银槎

朱碧山银槎（chá）是一件白银制成的酒杯，为元代著名银匠朱碧山的代表作品。槎即木筏，在中国古代传说中，可以乘槎穿越大海，寻访与之相连的天河，是很多作品的灵感来源。

酒杯被铸成形似老树的槎状，中空以贮酒，一位道人倚坐槎上，束发宽袍，须眉皓然，正凝视手中书卷。槎底部刻有“贮玉液而自畅”“知得酒中趣，方留世上名”等诗句，表达饮酒之趣。槎尾正面刻有“龙槎”二字，背面则刻槎杯的制作年代、制作地点和作者等。此杯运用了多种制作工艺，主体为铸

槎尾正面的“龙槎”二字

The front of the tail carved with the Chinese characters “龙槎” (*long cha*), literally “Dragon Raft”.

Silver Raft-Shaped Cup by Zhu Bishan

The silver raft-shaped wine cup was created by Zhu Bishan, an eminent silversmith in the Yuan Dynasty. In Chinese mythology, one could take a wooden raft across the sea and reach the heavenly river, and this means of transport has inspired many art and craft works.

The wine cup was crafted in the shape of a raft resembling an old tree. The hollow part was used to store wine. A Taoist wearing a loose robe and with his hair tied up, who has long beard and eyebrows, sits on the raft while gazing at a book in his hand. The bottom of the silver raft was engraved with verses such as “Storing jade liquid and feeling free” and “Knowing the fun of wine, leaving a name in the world” to express the joy of drinking.

The front of the tail is carved with the Chinese characters “龙槎 (*long cha*)”, literally meaning “Dragon Raft”, and the back is etched with its year and place of production as well as the name of its creator.

主体形象
The figure adorning the silver raft-shaped wine cup.

成后雕刻，人物的头、手、云履等则是铸成后接焊，成品浑然一体，丝毫不显焊接痕迹。现存于世的朱碧山银槎仅有 4 件，另外 3 件分别藏于台北故宫博物院、吴文化博物馆和美国克利夫兰艺术博物馆。

这件银槎构思巧妙，技艺精湛，兼具中国绘画与雕塑的特点，代表了元代铸银工艺的高超水平。

The production process for this cup involved a variety of techniques. The main body was carved after casting, and the head, hands, and shoes of the figure were cast and then welded together with other parts. The finished artifact looks flawless, without any welding traces.

Only four silver raft-shaped cups attributed to Zhu Bishan have survived to this day, and the other three are respectively housed in the Palace Museum in Taipei, the Museum of Wu in Suzhou, east China's Jiangsu Province, and the Cleveland Museum of Art in the United States.

This silver raft-shaped cup boasts ingenious design and superb craftsmanship and combines the characteristics of Chinese painting and sculpture, representing the high level of silver casting techniques in the Yuan Dynasty.

四

明清时期宫廷精品

故宫博物院珍藏着大量明清时期的宫廷文物，这些文物精品不仅工艺精湛、材质名贵，更展现出当时工匠们的创新精神。从精致细腻的雕漆图盒到艳丽明快的斗彩瓷器，从庄重典雅的室内家具到巧夺天工的玉山文玩，每件作品都凝聚了匠人的智慧与汗水，作为宫廷艺术的典范，反映出当时社会的审美趣味，承载着中华民族的基因和血脉，成为中华优秀传统文化传承与创新的见证。

ROYAL COLLECTION OF THE MING AND QING DYNASTIES

The Palace Museum boasts a large collection of court relics from the Ming and Qing dynasties. The relics not only feature superb craftsmanship and precious materials, but also showcase the innovative spirit of the craftsmen of past times.

Each relic embodies the wisdom and hard work of the craftsmen—from the delicately carved lacquer boxes to the gorgeous and brightly colored *doucai* porcelain (a variety of decorative porcelain formed by the combination of underglaze blue-and-white and overglaze decoration), from the solemn and elegant interior furniture to the ingenious jade carvings.

As masterpieces of court art, they reflect the aesthetic taste of Chinese society in various periods, carry the cultural genes of the Chinese nation, and bear witness to the inheritance and innovation of fine traditional Chinese culture.

永乐雕漆（剔红双龙牡丹纹圆盒）

剔红双龙牡丹纹圆盒为明永乐时期（1403—1424）的漆器。盒盖正中雕有双龙戏珠图案，以牡丹纹衬底，纹饰空隙间布满精细的菱花锦纹。

盒盖采用漆雕工艺，即在胎表层层刷漆，积累到一定厚度后再雕刻花纹。所用漆色有红、黄、绿、黑等，也可交替叠刷。常见的红色漆雕被称为剔红。明成祖朱棣酷爱雕漆器，曾在皇城内建立御用漆器作坊，汇集地方名匠，专门生产雕漆器。他在位期间制作的永乐雕漆，刷漆层数明显增多，可达一二百层，

Yongle Lacquer Carving (Carved Cinnabar Lacquer Circular Box with Double-Dragon and Peony Patterns)

The carved cinnabar lacquer circular box with double-dragon and peony patterns dates back to Emperor Yongle's reign (1403-1424) of the Ming Dynasty. The center of the box cover is carved with two dragons playing with a pearl, with peony patterns as the background, surrounded by diamond decorative motifs.

The cover was crafted with the lacquer carving technique: Lacquer is repeatedly applied on the surface of the object, and then patterns are carved after the lacquer reaches a certain thickness. The most commonly used lacquer colors are red, yellow, green, and black, which can also be applied alternately. Common red lacquerware is called cinnabar lacquer carving.

Zhu Di (1360-1424), Emperor Yongle of the Ming Dynasty, loved carved lacquerwares. He established a royal lacquerware workshop in the imperial city and recruited famous craftsmen from around the country to produce carved lacquerwares.

During his reign, the layers of lacquer applied increased significantly, up to 100-200 layers, and the thickness could reach about 1.5 centimeters. Carved lacquerwares of the Yongle reign boast exquisite carving and multi-layered and stereoscopic decorative patterns, which have been highly acclaimed by later generations.

厚度可达 1.5 厘米上下。永乐雕漆雕工精美，花纹层次丰富，立体感强，受到后人的广泛推崇。清代乾隆皇帝钟爱永乐雕漆，曾下令在新制的雕漆器上镌刻永乐款。

此漆盒漆层肥厚，图案边缘圆润光滑，不露棱角和刀刻痕迹，装饰风格及龙纹具备永乐雕漆的标准特征，代表了明代永乐雕漆的最高水平。

Emperor Qianlong of the Qing Dynasty loved carved lacquerwares of the Yongle reign so much that he ordered the mark "Yongle" be engraved on newly carved lacquerwares.

This box features a thick layer of lacquer. The edges of the patterns are smoothly polished, concealing the carving traces. The decorative style and dragon patterns are typical of carved lacquerwares of the Yongle reign, representing the highest level of lacquer carving at that time.

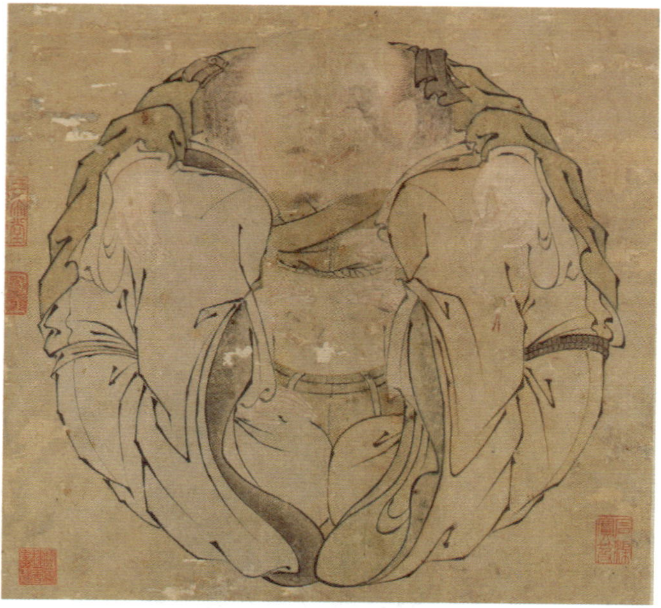

画心

The main part of the painting *A Full Circle of Harmony.*

《一团和气图》

《一团和气图》是明宪宗朱见深 19 岁时所作的一幅人物画。

画中所绘看似一位盘腿而坐的笑弥勒，细看却是三人合一。左为头戴道冠的老者，右为头戴方巾的儒生，二人各执经卷，面面相接，构成第三人。第三人手搭二人肩头，为佛门中人，手捻佛珠。朱见深还在画上题下《御制一团和气图赞》，引用“虎溪三笑”的故事。相传惠远法师在虎溪边修佛，送客不过溪。一日，儒门之秀陶潜与道士陆修静来访，相谈甚欢，相送时不觉过溪，三人大笑而别。朱见深以此为灵感，用诙谐的人物造型传达了儒、释、道“三教合一”的思想，也借此告诫朝野摒弃纷争、团结一心，共创国泰民安。

这幅画体现出作者纯熟的绘画技艺，更以绝妙的构思彰显了中华文明自古以来尊重差异、和谐共处的价值理念。

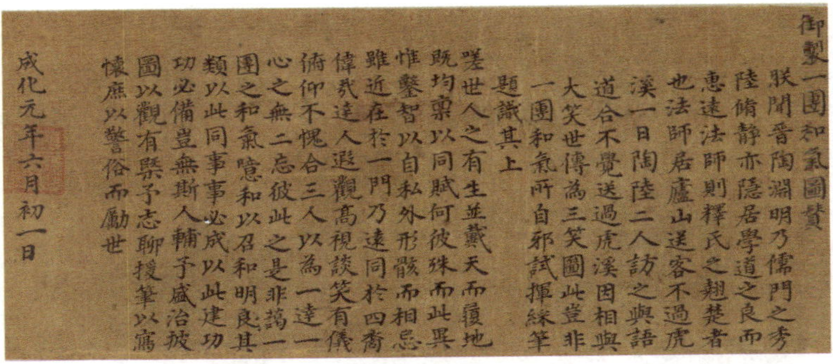
御製一團和氣圖贊
朕聞晉陶淵明乃儒門之秀陸脩靜亦隱居學道之良而惠遠法師則釋氏之翹楚者也法師居廬山送客不過虎溪一日陶陸二人訪之與語道合不覺送過虎溪因相與大笑世傳為三笑圖此豈非一團和氣所自邪試揮綵筆題識其上
嗟世人之有生並戴天而履地既均稟以同賦何彼殊而此異惟鑿智以自私外形骸而相忌雖近在於一門乃遠同於四裔偉哉達人遐觀高視談笑有儀俯仰不愧合三人以為一達一心之無二忘彼此之是非藹一團之和氣噫和以召和明良其類以此同事事必成以此建功功必備豈無斯人輔予盛治披圖以觀有契予志聊援筆以寫懷庶以警俗而勵世
成化元年六月初一日

《御制一团和气图赞》

"Ode to *A Full Circle of Harmony* by the Emperor" on the painting.

A Full Circle of Harmony

A Full Circle of Harmony is a figure painting by Zhu Jianshen (1447-1487), at the age of 19, during the reign of Emperor Xianzong of the Ming Dynasty.

At first sight, the painting depicts a smiling Maitreya Buddha sitting cross-legged, but on closer inspection, it is a trio in one. On the left is an old man wearing a Taoist crown, and on the right is a Confucian scholar wrapping his hair with a handkerchief. Standing face to face, the duo hold a handscroll together. The Maitreya in the middle hugs the other two with his arms around their shoulders, his left hand holding a string of Buddhist prayer beads.

Zhu Jianshen inscribed "Ode to *A Full Circle of Harmony* by the Emperor" on the painting, quoting the story of "Three Laughs at Tiger Brook". Legend holds that Master Hui Yuan practiced Buddhism in seclusion by the Tiger Brook and would seldom cross the brook when seeing off guests.

One day, Tao Qian, a renowned Confucian scholar, and Lu Xiujing, a Taoist priest, visited Hui Yuan, and the three had a good time. Deeply engrossed in conversation, Hui Yuan didn't even realize he had passed the brook when seeing off his guests. The trio laughed upon realizing this.

Inspired by this story, Zhu Jianshen created this painting with a witty style, conveying the idea of integrating Confucianism, Buddhism, and Taoism and expressing the hope that all strata of society would discard disputes and unite as one to build a prosperous country and create a peaceful life for the people.

This painting not only reflects the painter's superb skills, but also manifests long-standing Chinese values of respecting diversity and seeking harmonious coexistence.

犀角器（鲍天成款犀角雕螭纹执壶）

犀角雕螭纹执壶，为明末江苏一带雕刻能手鲍天成所制。他擅雕牙角材质，作品多进入宫廷。犀角珍贵且尺寸小，鲜少用于制壶，此壶几乎没有使用痕迹，应为文玩。

壶有盔帽状的壶盖，可以打开。壶身纹饰分四层，两层为蟠夔纹，兽面纹、蕉叶纹各一层。出水口和壶把均有螭龙围绕。犀角制品大多不记录制作者，此壶底有“鲍天成制”款识，属难得佳作。

“鲍天成制”底款

The inscriptions “Made by Bao Tiancheng” on the bottom of the rhino horn-carved ewer.

Rhino Horn Artifact (Rhino Horn-Carved Ewer with Dragon Patterns by Bao Tiancheng)

The rhino horn-carved ewer was made by Bao Tiancheng, a renowned sculptor in Jiangsu during the late Ming Dynasty. Bao excelled in ivory and horn carving, and many of his works were collected in the imperial palace. Precious and small, rhino horns were hardly ever used to make ewers and pots. There is no sign that this ewer was ever used for its purpose, so it has been conjectured that the artifact was made as a collectible curio.

The ewer has a helmet-shaped lid that can be opened. Four circles of decorations surround its body including two circles of dragon patterns, one circle of animal face patterns, and another circle of banana leaf patterns. The spout and handle are also covered by dragon patterns. Most of the rhino horn products have no signs to identify their makers. However, the bottom of this exquisite ewer is carved with the inscriptions “Made by Bao Tiancheng”.

打开的鲍天成款犀角雕螭纹执壶

The unlidded rhino horn-carved ewer with dragon patterns by Bao Tiancheng.

这只犀角壶曾流失海外，为香港爱国收藏家叶义捐赠。叶义先生祖籍广东，是香港有名的外科医生。他业余爱好收藏，尤其喜欢竹木牙角类文物。20 世纪 80 年代叶义访京，与故宫文物专家杨伯达相识，达成捐赠意向。可惜意向还未实现，叶义便骤然病逝。其香港友人受托执行遗嘱，于 1985 年 1 月将他收藏的 81 件犀角器悉数捐赠故宫博物院。

这批犀角器的到来，不仅大大丰富了故宫博物院此类文物的馆藏数量，亦是香港收藏家拳拳爱国之心的见证。

This rhino horn-carved ewer was once lost abroad. Eventually, Yip Yi (1919-1984), a patriotic collector in Hong Kong, donated it to the Palace Museum.

Originally from Guangdong, Yip became a well-known surgeon in Hong Kong. He developed a hobby of collecting relics, especially bamboo, wood, and horn artifacts. In the 1980s, Yip visited Beijing and met Yang Boda, a cultural heritage expert at the Palace Museum, to whom Yip expressed his donation intention but suddenly died of illness before the donation was made. In January 1985, the executors of his will in Hong Kong donated all 81 rhino horn artifacts in his collection to the Palace Museum.

The rhino horn artifacts donated by Yip had significantly enriched the collection of similar relics in the Palace Museum, and testified to the Hong Kong collector's allegiance to the motherland.

宣德炉（铜冲耳乳足炉）

宣德炉是继商周青铜器之后，中国铜器铸造工艺的又一个高峰。

宣德炉，原指明代宣德年间宫廷铸造的铜质香炉，因炉底铸有“大明宣德年制”印款而得名。后经历代仿制，凡形制、款识与之相近的铜炉均获此名。《宣德鼎彝谱》载，明宣德三年（1428），暹罗国王向中国进献数万斤精炼铜料，色如黄金，称“风磨铜”。明宣宗下旨，依此铜料，仿照商周青铜礼器及宋代名窑瓷器，铸造供祭祀和陈设用的皇家铜器 3365 件。舶来的原料、天子的旨意、经典的蓝本和精确的记述，令宣德炉成为传奇。

这件铜冲耳乳足炉，两耳三足、腹部浑圆，仿宋代哥窑三足炉，为宣德炉经典造型。炉壁经长年积累，包浆厚实，可见曾在宫中长期使用。

如今明代宣德时期所造铜炉极为罕见。这件铜炉属清宫旧藏，也是故宫博物院所藏唯一一件明代宣德时期铸造的传世珍品。

Xuande Incense Burner (Three-Legged Copper Censer with Upright Ears)

The Xuande incense burners represented another pinnacle of Chinese copper casting technology after the bronze wares of the Shang and Zhou dynasties.

The Xuande incense burners refer to copper censers made by the royal court during Emperor Xuande's reign of the Ming Dynasty. They derived the name from the mark "Made during Xuande's reign of the Ming Dynasty" usually found on the bottom. Later copper censers modeled after this shape, style, and mark were also so named.

According to an ancient monograph on the incense burners of Xuande's reign, in 1428, the king of Siam sent several tons of refined copper as tribute to the Ming emperor. This kind of refined copper material, called "*fengmotong*" (literally "wind-milled copper"), glimmered like gold.

Emperor Xuande decreed to use the material to cast 3,365 royal bronze wares for sacrificial ceremonies and ornaments, in imitation of the bronze ritual instruments of the Shang and Zhou dynasties and porcelain wares from famous kilns in the Song Dynasty.

The incense burners of Xuande's reign, made with imported material upon the emperor's decree and modeled after classic utensils, became everlasting legends based on the descriptions preserved in ancient books.

This three-legged copper censer with two upright ears and a round belly was modeled after the style of the three-legged porcelain censers from the Ge Kiln in the Song Dynasty, a typical design of the incense burners of Xuande's reign. After centuries of weathering, the censer formed a thick coating due to oxidation, indicating that it was long used in the imperial palace.

Only a few copper censers made during Xuande's reign have been preserved to this day. From the collection of the Qing court, this censer is the only of its kind cast in the Xuande's reign in the Palace Museum.

铜冲耳乳足炉底部款识

Inscriptions on the bottom of the three-legged copper censer with upright ears.

凤冠（正面）
The front side of the phoenix crown.

凤冠（点翠嵌珍珠宝石金龙凤冠）

点翠嵌珍珠宝石金龙凤冠，1956年出土于北京明定陵，凤冠主人是万历皇帝的孝靖皇后。

凤冠是皇后在接受册封、祭祀祖先、参加朝会时所佩戴的冠冕。此凤冠以涂漆细竹丝编制，在此基础上，通体如意云片皆使用翠鸟羽毛装饰，称为点翠工艺。点翠工艺十分复杂，需要先以金属制成特定的架子，再用金属线勾勒出纹样轮廓，然后在线条间的凹陷处粘贴翠鸟羽毛。

凤冠（背面）

The rear side of the phoenix crown.

Phoenix Crown (Adorned with Kingfisher Feathers, Pearls, Gemstones, and Gold Dragons)

The phoenix crown adorned with kingfisher feathers, pearls, gemstones and gold dragons was unearthed in 1956 from the Dingling Tomb of the Ming Dynasty in Beijing. It belonged to Empress Xiaojing, wife of Emperor Wanli.

Phoenix crown refers to the ceremonial headgear worn by the empress when she accepted canonization, worshipped her ancestors, and participated in court meetings. This one is made of lacquered fine bamboo wires adorned with kingfisher feathers in the shape of auspicious clouds.

This technique is known as Diancui. The process is very complex: Craftsmen need to first weave a specially designed metal framework, then form the outlines of decorative patterns with metal wires, and finally paste kingfisher feathers onto the recesses between the lines.

口衔珠宝流苏金龙装饰

Gold dragons holding jewels and tassels in their mouths decorating the phoenix crown.

这些如意云片，毛丝细密，有丝绢光泽。凤冠共镶嵌红蓝宝石一百多颗，珍珠五千余粒。冠顶部等距离排列着金丝编制的金龙三条，其中左右两条口衔珠宝流苏。冠前部有两只对称的翠蓝色凤凰，凤凰展翅呈飞翔状，栩栩如生。冠后部有一对"博鬓"（古代妇女头饰，也用于展示身份地位），上镶珍珠、宝石，以扇形向左右分开。冠口一周镶嵌花朵，由红蓝宝石及小米珠组成。

凤冠将生物之灵与装饰之美结合，体现了中国匠人高超的手工艺技能。

翠蓝色凤凰装饰

A turquoise blue phoenix decoration.

These cloud-shaped ornaments feature fine hairs and a silky luster. The phoenix crown is inlaid with more than 100 rubies and sapphires as well as over 5,000 pearls. Everything on top of the crown is evenly distributed.

Three gold dragons were crafted with gold wires, of which the left and right hold jewels and tassels in their mouths. Two lifelike emerald-blue phoenixes were symmetrically arranged in the front part of the crown, which spread their wings as if they were flying.

At the back of the crown is a pair of *bobin* (headdress worn by women in ancient China to show their social status), which are inlaid with pearls and gemstones and stretch toward two sides like an unfolding fan. The crown brim is inset with flowers made of rubies, sapphires, and tiny pearls.

Combining the beauty of living beings and decorative motifs, the phoenix crown embodies the superb skills of Chinese craftsmen.

德化窑白瓷观音像

这件德化窑白瓷观音像烧造于明代，材质坚细洁白，釉色莹亮温润。观音发髻高盘，头戴兜帽，双目微闭，似乎面带笑意，神态端庄慈祥。身着高腰长裙，法衣轻盈飘动，胸前珠饰光润，双手藏在袖子里，光脚站在海浪之上。观音像背后有明代后期最为著名的德化窑瓷工何朝宗的戳记。

德化窑址在今福建省德化县，自明代起主烧白瓷，以达摩、观音等人物像最为突出。德化窑瓷质优异，胎釉浑然一体，色泽光润明亮如脂似玉，洁白中闪现牙黄，自古享誉国内外，称为“中国白”。这件德化窑白瓷观音像便是中国白瓷的典型代表。

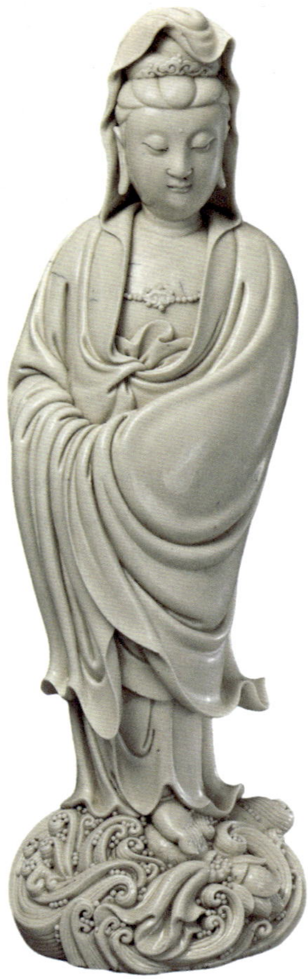

观音像胸部细节

A close-up of the chest of the Avalokitesvara statue.

观音像足部细节

A close-up of the feet of the Avalokitesvara statue.

White Porcelain Avalokitesvara Statue by the Dehua Kiln

This white porcelain Avalokitesvara statue was produced in the Dehua Kiln during the Ming Dynasty. It boasts fine, white, and bright glaze. The Avalokitesvara has a high bun and wears a hood, with her eyes slightly closed. She seems to be smiling, demonstrating a dignified, amicable demeanor.

She is dressed in a high-waisted long skirt, and her robe seems light and fluttering. The pearl jewel she wears on the chest is lustrous, and her hands are hidden in the sleeves. She stands barefoot above the waves.

On the back of the statue is the mark of He Chaozong, the most famous porcelain craftsman at the Dehua Kiln during the late Ming Dynasty.

The site of the Dehua Kiln is in Dehua County, southeast China's Fujian Province today. Since the Ming Dynasty, the kiln had been committed to producing white porcelain, especially porcelain figurines such as Bodhidharma and Avalokitesvara.

White porcelain from the Dehua Kiln features high-quality materials and lustrous glaze as bright and warm as jade, with ivory yellowish color brimming in white. It has been well-known globally since ancient times, earning the reputation "Blanc de Chine", or "white from China". This white porcelain Avalokitesvara statue from the Dehua Kiln is a masterpiece of Chinese white porcelain.

成化斗彩鸡缸杯

明代成化斗彩以鸡缸杯最为著名。鸡缸杯造型小巧，胎薄体轻，装饰清新。杯内光素，杯外花叶山石间，雄鸡昂首啼鸣，雌鸡低头觅食，小鸡欢快展翅，相互追逐，整体画面虽静犹动。

斗彩，是明代成化年间创烧的新品种。制法上，先用青料勾画轮廓，上釉高温烧成，形成釉下青花轮廓，再按轮廓线于釉上施彩料，低温固色，使釉下彩与釉上彩争奇斗艳。这件鸡缸杯，画面上蓝、绿、黄、红、黑等相映成辉，平涂、勾线、染彩等技法相得益彰。浓淡之间，素雅、鲜丽兼而有之。

此杯为景德镇御窑厂烧制，专供御用。文献记载，万历皇帝御前曾有成化斗彩鸡缸杯一对，价值颇高。明清以来，鸡缸杯仿烧不断，是当之无愧的一代名瓷。

Chenghua *Doucai* Chicken Cup

Chicken cups are the most famous representatives of *doucai* porcelain wares made during Emperor Chenghua's reign (1465-1487) of the Ming Dynasty.

This exquisite chicken cup features a thin wall and refreshing decorations. It lacks any motifs inside. On the outer surface of the cup, amidst plants and rocks, a rooster crows while lifting his neck high, a hen bows her head to forage, and several chicks spread their wings happily and chase each other, giving the entire image an air of vigor and movement.

The *doucai* porcelain is a new variety created during the Ming Dynasty. Craftsmen first drew outlines with cobalt blue and applied the glaze before burning the objects at high temperature to form the underglaze blue and white outlines. Then, they applied colors above the glaze according to the outlines and fixed the colors at low temperature. The underglaze and overglaze colors compete with each other, hence the name *doucai* (literally, "contending colors").

This chicken cup combines colors like blue, green, yellow, red, and black, and involves techniques such as painting, outlining, and dyeing, integrating elegance with brilliance.

The cup was from the Jingdezhen Imperial Kiln, which was committed to producing porcelain utensils for royal use. Historical records show that Emperor Wanli owned a pair of valuable Chenghua *doucai* chicken cups. The Ming and Qing dynasties saw many imitations of famous Chenghua *doucai* chicken cups.

填漆戗金琴桌

填漆戗金琴桌，明万历年制，长 97 厘米，宽 45 厘米，高 70 厘米。琴桌长方形，通体红漆，桌面正中开光（为突出形象，在器物上勾勒出一个空间，如矩形，在其内饰以图纹），以戗金绘双龙戏珠（戗金：即在器物表面刻出花纹，再在刻纹内施以金胶、金粉，呈现出金色的花纹），四周赶珠龙纹与八宝纹间隔出现。牙板及桌腿亦饰龙纹。

琴桌专为弹奏古琴而制作，看似普通，却暗藏玄机。此琴桌底部设挡板，挡板上有镂空钱纹两个，挡板与桌面之间存在几厘米空隙，形成共鸣箱。弹奏古琴时，琴声在共鸣箱内振动共鸣，由镂空钱纹孔传出。这样的设计，提升了琴的音色和音效，很是巧妙。

中国古代，文人崇尚清雅的生活方式，抚琴作乐便是雅事之一。好琴搭配合适的琴桌，才能尽可能发挥出琴音之妙。这件琴桌集精湛工艺、华丽造型和实用设计于一体，是明万历时期的艺术佳作。

填漆戗金琴桌 - 桌面

The top of the gold painted lacquer *guqin* table.

Gold Painted Lacquer *Guqin* Table

The gold painted lacquer *guqin* table, dating back to the reign of Emperor Wanli of the Ming Dynasty, measures 97 centimeters in length, 45 centimeters in width, and 70 centimeters in height. The rectangular table is entirely painted with red lacquer, with *kaiguang* (a geometric shape such as a rectangle outlined on the surface of an object, decorated with patterns on the insides) in the middle of its top.

The table is adorned with two dragons playing a pearl drawn with *qiangjin* (a technique to engrave patterns on the surface of an object and then apply gold glue or powder to create golden motifs). Surrounding the main image are patterns of dragons chasing a pearl as well as patterns of the eight treasures. The edges and legs of the table are also decorated with dragon patterns.

The table was made for playing the *guqin*. It appears to be fairly mundane, but in fact, many details were skillfully designed. At the bottom of the table is a baffle plate with two hollowed-out coin-shaped patterns. A centimeters-wide space between the baffle plate and the tabletop creates a resonance box. When the *guqin* is played on the table, its sound vibrates through the resonance box and is amplified by the hollowed-out coin-shaped patterns. This ingenious design can enhance the timbre and acoustic effect of the *guqin*.

In ancient China, the literati advocated an elegant lifestyle, and playing the *guqin* was considered a graceful pastime. A fine musical instrument can generate better sound in tandem with a suitable table. A masterpiece of furniture in the period of Emperor Wanli of the Ming Dynasty, this table integrates exquisite craftsmanship, ornate shapes, and practical design.

东珠朝珠

在清代，东珠朝珠只有皇帝、皇太后和皇后在参加盛大典礼时才能佩戴，既是装饰，又能彰显身份。

东珠朝珠的特殊性体现在其主要材料东珠上。所谓东珠，是生长于清代统治者家乡，即中国东北地区河流中的淡水珍珠。东珠成为清代统治者家族发源地的象征，采集和使用都受到极其严格的监管。

这盘东珠朝珠主体部分由108颗东珠串成，这些珍珠被蓝色的蓝晶石珠和橘红色的珊瑚珠隔成4等份，象征一年的四季。朝珠上的3串珠串称为“记念”，每串记念由10颗小珠子串成，象征一个月的上、中、下三旬，每旬10天。朝珠上由长带子串联的垂坠为背云，朝珠佩戴时背云垂在颈后，可以避免朝珠移转错位。

朝珠的设计饱含人们对节气、时间及自然的理解。东珠朝珠地位尊贵，更突显出中国人对祖先和家乡的尊崇。

东珠朝珠

A set of court beads made of East Pearls.

东珠朝珠装在匣中，黄条上书文宗显皇帝，即咸丰皇帝

A set of court beads made of East Pearls in a container, with a yellow silk strip carrying the name of Emperor Wenzong Xian, also known as Emperor Xianfeng.

A Set of East Pearl Court Beads

In the Qing Dynasty, only the emperor, empress dowager, and empress could wear court beads made of East Pearls when attending important ceremonies, as both accessories and a symbol of dignity.

The uniqueness of such court beads lies in their primary materials—East Pearls. They are freshwater pearls from rivers in northeast China, the homeland of Qing rulers. As a symbol of the birthplace of the Qing royal family, the collection and use of such pearls were under strict supervision.

This set of court beads consists of 108 East Pearls, evenly separated into four sections by blue kyanite beads and orange coral beads, symbolizing the four seasons. The three short strings of beads, known as *jinian*, each featuring 10 pearls, symbolizing the three 10-day periods of a month. The pendant connected by a long belt with the beads is called "*beiyun*" (literally "back cloud") and placed behind the neck to prevent dislocation.

The design of court beads conveys ancient Chinese understanding of seasons, time, and nature. The dignified status of East Pearls bespeaks Chinese veneration for their ancestral roots.

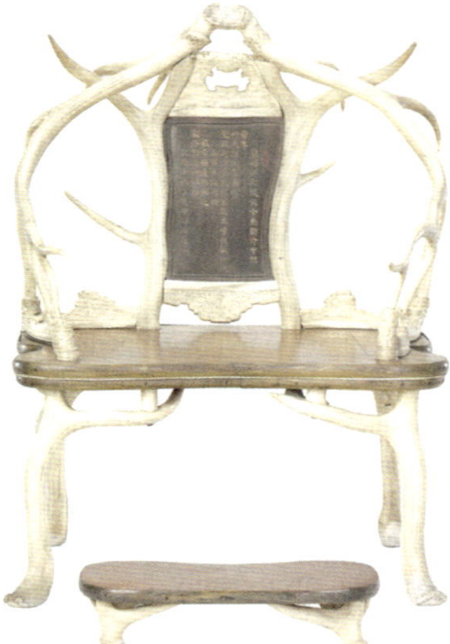

鹿角椅

鹿角椅，是以鹿角搭配不同材质的座面和背板制作而成的极具清宫特色的椅式。所用鹿角皆取自狩猎所获之鹿，样式按照明式圈椅设计，造型威武霸气。

这把康熙朝的鹿角椅，座面外沿一圈勒象牙线，前沿和两侧微内凹。座面嵌骨雕勾云纹坐牙，与鹿角圈背连接。椅脚为两只鹿的支角，角叉对称向里，形成支撑。椅背刻有乾隆皇帝的御制诗，证实此椅为康熙帝亲猎之鹿角所制。椅前另附脚踏，

座面嵌骨雕勾云纹坐牙
The seat surface decorated with bone-carved cloud patterns.

Antler Chair

The antler chair, with its seat surface and back made of different materials, boasts the distinctive style of the Qing court. All the antlers used were collected by hunting. In the style of Ming-dynasty round-backed armchairs, it displays a majestic and imposing appeal.

This antler chair dates back to Emperor Kangxi's reign (1662-1722). The outer edge of the seat is inlaid with a line made of ivory, and the front and left and right sides are slightly concave. The seat surface is decorated with bone-carved cloud patterns, which is connected with the round back made of antlers. Its legs are made of two antlers that point inward symmetrically to support the chair. The back of the chair is engraved with a poem by Emperor

乾隆皇帝御制诗

The back of the chair engraved with a poem by Emperor Qianlong.

脚踏的四足为小鹿的鹿角。国内现存鹿角椅七件，一件在沈阳故宫博物院，一件在内蒙古自治区博物馆，其余五件均藏于故宫博物院，其中三件为康熙朝制作，两件为乾隆朝制作。

鹿角椅将鹿角的自然形态与椅子的造型及功能巧妙结合，显示出工匠大胆的创新设计和高超的制作工艺，成为清代特有的家具品种。

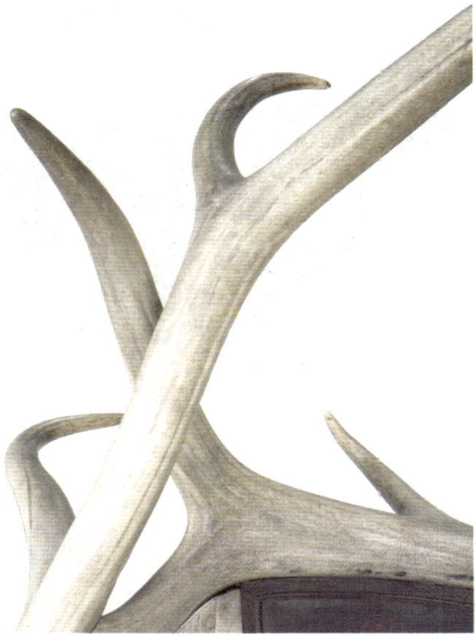

鹿角椅圈背

The round back of the antler chair.

Qianlong, which verified that the antlers came from deer hunted by Emperor Kangxi. A footstool in front of the chair features four legs made of the antlers of a fawn.

Only seven such antler chairs have been preserved in China, with one housed in the Shenyang Palace Museum, one in the Inner Mongolia Museum, and the remaining five in the Palace Museum, of which, three were made during the reign of Emperor Kangxi and two during the reign of Emperor Qianlong (1736-1796).

A unique furniture variety in the Qing Dynasty, these chairs skillfully combine the natural form of antlers with the function of chairs, demonstrating bold, innovative design and superb craftsmanship.

松花石暖砚

松花石暖砚由砚与承托砚的掐丝珐琅盒共同组成。中国东北的松花江是清代祖先发祥地，由此地江石制成的砚，专供清代皇室御用。石砚四周雕琢螭纹，砚体呈青绿色，质地细腻，色泽淡雅。砚上一侧雕荷叶形墨池，用于盛放清水或墨汁，池边有水孔，向内注水可防止砚石加热时开裂。砚堂表面凹陷，应为长久研墨所致。

此砚配有掐丝珐琅螭龙纹砚盒，掐丝线条工整，蓝色掐丝珐琅部位，饰以螭龙、寿桃，堪称佳品。盒周装饰铜鎏金錾花镂空螭纹。冬日寒冷，为防止研墨结冰，盒内可燃炭，空气通过盒周镂空处流通，保证炭火不熄。盒底部镌刻“康熙年制”。

暖砚与砚盒，不即不离，浑然一体，其设计理念之奇巧、制造工艺之精良，令人叹为观止。中国古代工匠之竭尽巧思，于此可见一斑。

底部镌刻

Inscriptions engraved on the bottom of the inkstone.

Songhua Warm Inkstone

The set of Songhua warm inkstone consists of an inkstone made of Songhua stone and a cloisonné box used to support the inkstone. The Songhua River Basin in northeast China was the ancestral homeland of Qing-dynasty rulers, and inkstones made of stone from the river were exclusive to the Qing royal court.

Carved with dragon patterns, this inkstone features delicate texture and elegant blue-green color. On one side of the inkstone, an engraved lotus leaf-shaped pool was used to hold water or ink. Water was injected into a hole on the edge of the pool to prevent the inkstone from cracking when heated. The surface of the inkstone has become depressed due to long-time usage.

The inkstone is equipped with a cloisonné box with dragon patterns, which features neat filigree lines. The blue cloisonné enamel part was decorated with dragon and peach patterns, making it a masterpiece of Chinese cloisonné. The box was decorated with hollowed-out copper gilt motifs. To prevent the ink from freezing in cold winter, charcoal was burned inside the box, and the hollowed-out parts allowed air to circulate, sustaining the burning of the charcoal. The bottom of the box was engraved with the mark "Made in the Kangxi reign".

The inkstone and the box are inseparable and boast ingenious design and superb craftsmanship, testifying to the wit of ancient Chinese craftsmen.

正面

The front of the court robe.

明黄色缎绣金龙朝袍

明黄色缎绣金龙朝袍制于清乾隆年间，身长 144 厘米，两袖通长 190 厘米。朝袍，是帝后在盛大典礼、祭祀活动时穿用的礼服之一。

此件为皇帝朝袍，绣金龙四十余条，造型丰富，细腻灵动。胸前、背后的正龙，瞠目张口，十分威严。绣金龙所用的“金线”，并非染制得来，而是将金箔切成细丝，捻绕于丝线芯上，以此绣龙，呈现出龙鳞闪闪的效果。此外，朝袍上绣十二章纹中的山、龙、华虫（雉鸡）、黼（fǔ）、黻（fú）等，象征帝王美德。这始于对舜、禹的歌颂，明清时期逐渐成为帝王礼服和吉服的专用纹样，但多数情况下十二章纹并不绣全。

Yellow Satin Court Robe Embroidered with Golden Dragons

The yellow satin court robe embroidered with golden dragons dates back to Emperor Qianlong's reign of the Qing Dynasty. It is 144 centimeters in body length, and its sleeves are 190 centimeters long. Court robes were ceremonial garments worn by the emperor and empresses on important occasions such as sacrificial ceremonies.

This robe was for the emperor, embroidered with more than 40 lifelike golden dragons in diverse shapes. The forward-looking dragons on the chest and the back look majestic. The threads used to embroider the golden dragons are not pure fabric, but fine gold wires twisted on silk threads, so the scales of the dragons glisten with golden luster.

In addition, the robe is adorned with the "twelve ornaments", such as mountains, dragons, pheasants, axes, and bows, which symbolize the emperor's virtues. The "twelve ornaments" were initially used to praise legendary ancient rulers Shun and Yu and gradually evolved into exclusive patterns to decorate imperial apparel for ceremonial and sacrificial occasions in the Ming and Qing dynasties. In most cases, not all the "twelve ornaments" were embroidered on the garments.

背面

The back of the court robe.

清代朝袍具有鲜明的满族服饰特点，如形似满弓的披肩领、马蹄袖等，均彰显其骑射习俗。清代统治者入主中原后，在接纳中国传统汉文化的同时，也保留了自身的民族特色，反映出中华民族自古以来就是多民族共同体，具有突出的统一性。

The court robes of the Qing Dynasty had distinctive features of Manchu costumes such as bow-shaped tippet collars and horseshoe-shaped sleeves, all of which hearkened back to the Manchu traditions of horse riding and archery. After the rulers of the Qing Dynasty came to power in the Central Plains region, they embraced traditional Han culture while retaining their Manchu lifestyles. As such, China has been a unified multi-ethnic nation since ancient times.

象牙席

象牙席，是用特制药水将象牙浸泡软化后，沿其本身纹理劈成细丝，再按照“人字纹”交错编织而成的席。

故宫博物院藏有两张象牙席，均为清代广东官员进贡之物。其一在建院前夕清点文物时已登记在册，其二则直到半个世纪后的 1978 年，在整理库房时意外发现。当时，工作人员发觉一捆草席偏重，打开后看到其中藏着白色席面。经过与在册文物的比对，确认白色席面正是罕见的象牙席。

席本是竹制居多，用象牙做席，是清朝大臣为皇帝准备礼物的奇思异想。虽有一时欢心，但雍正皇帝认为“好用此物”会上行下效，引起奢靡之风，便明确下旨，禁止广东地区工匠再制作、官员再进献象牙编织品。

如今，中国政府已明令禁止捕猎野生象和交易象牙及其制品。象牙加工技艺转而使用牛骨等易得材料继续传承。

象牙席一角

A corner of the ivory mat.

象牙席面编织细节

A close-up of weaving textures of the ivory mat.

Ivory Mat

Ivory mats were woven in a staggered manner with wires made of ivory softened with a special liquid and then split into filaments according to its natural texture. Mats woven in this way featured herringbone patterns.

The Palace Museum has preserved two ivory mats, both of which were tributes from Guangdong officials during the Qing Dynasty. One was registered when relics were counted on the eve of the establishment of the museum, and the other was discovered by chance in 1978 when the museum rearranged the stock in its warehouse: A staff member noticed that a bundle of straw mats was heavier than expected, and when he opened it, a white mat hidden inside was brought to light. After comparing it with the registered relics, experts confirmed that it was a rare ivory mat.

Mats were mostly made of bamboo. Using ivory to weave mats was a whimsical idea from Qing-dynasty officials to prepare gifts for the emperor. Although momentarily pleased by the gift, Emperor Yongzheng believed that it could cause others to follow suit and seek extravagance, so he issued a decree to prohibit craftsmen in Guangdong from making ivory woven items and officials from presenting such tributes.

Today, the Chinese government has banned the hunting of wild elephants and trade of ivory and its products. Traditional ivory handicraft now continues to be passed on using easily available materials such as ox bones as substitutes.

大禹治水玉山

大禹治水玉山是故宫博物院所藏最大的单体玉雕，通高两米多，宽近一米，重达五吨。所用玉料采自新疆，为一整块和田玉。玉料运抵京城后，乾隆皇帝钦定以《大禹治水图》为题材，命人绘制玉山图纸，再依图纸分别做出蜡样和木样。扬州当时以擅作大件玉雕闻名于世，故将玉料沿大运河送抵扬州，依样雕刻完成后运回京城，前后耗

玉山正面

The front side of the jade carving.

Jade Carving *Yu the Great Harnesses the Floods*

Yu the Great Harnesses the Floods is the largest single jade carving in the collection of the Palace Museum. It is more than two meters high and nearly one meter wide and weighs five tons.

It was carved from a whole piece of Hetian nephrite mined from Xinjiang. After the jade material arrived in Beijing, Emperor Qianlong ordered a jade carving themed "Yu the Great Harnesses the Floods". He entrusted someone to draw the blueprint for the jade carving, according to which wax and wood molds were made.

Because Yangzhou was noted for making large jade carvings at that time, the material was floated to Yangzhou via the Grand Canal and transported back to the capital after the carving was completed. It took more than 10 years to complete the

玉山左侧面

The left side of the jade carving.

玉山右侧面

The right side of the jade carving.

时十余年。玉山被安放在乐寿堂中，至今二百余年未曾移动。

整座玉山展示了神助焚山、开山凿石、疏通水路等 11 个场景，共有持斧、构架、拉绳等 53 个人物。大禹在玉山正面中部，他高举大锤，仿佛马上要凿开一块顽石。玉山背面雕刻有乾隆皇帝御题诗文，歌颂了大禹治水的功绩，讲述了变玉石为玉山的过程，抒发了皇帝对平定西北、统一疆土后稳定发展的感慨。

大禹治水玉山既是中国古代玉雕工艺的登峰造极之作，也是中华民族齐心协力、不畏艰难的精神象征。

玉山背面乾隆御题诗文

The back of the jade carving engraved with inscriptions by Emperor Qianlong.

project. The jade carving has since been housed in the Hall of Joyful Longevity for over 200 years.

The entire jade carving depicts 11 scenes such as setting the mountains on fire with the help of gods, chiseling the mountains, and dredging the waterways, involving a total of 53 figures holding axes, building frames, and pulling ropes. Yu the Great stands in the center, holding a sledgehammer high as if to strike a hard stone.

The back of the jade carving was engraved with a poem by Emperor Qianlong to praise the achievements of Yu the Great in harnessing the floods, describe the process of making the jade carving, and express his feelings about the country's stable development after pacifying the northwestern border areas.

Yu the Great Harnesses the Floods represents the pinnacle of ancient Chinese jade carving and symbolizes the unity and hardworking spirit of the Chinese nation.

玉山正面

The front of the jade carving.

桐荫仕女玉山

桐荫仕女玉山为清乾隆年间的玉雕作品，由黄褐色带皮白玉制成。

玉山以月亮门为界，将庭院隔为内外。院外为玉雕正面，门右侧一位仕女手持灵芝而立，周围环绕桐荫和假山。院内为玉雕背面，背面左侧雕有芭蕉、石桌和石凳，右侧仕女手捧宝瓶，身姿款款。月亮门半开半合，虚掩遮映间透着光亮，好似两位仕女可以透过门缝对视交谈，给人以无限遐想。

玉山构思极为巧妙。用材原为雕去玉碗后的余料，玉匠巧妙地利用其形状特征，结合俏色工艺，即利用玉石原色，以中部空洞为门，以四周褐色玉皮为桐叶、芭蕉，创作出浑然天成

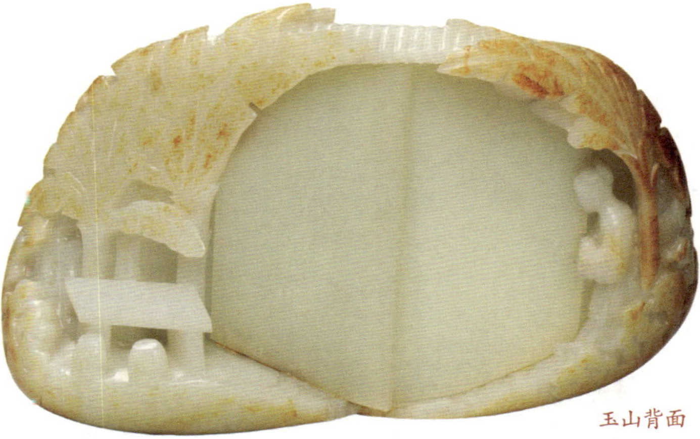

玉山背面

The back of the jade carving.

Jade Carving *Ladies Under a Chinese Parasol Tree*

The jade carving *Ladies Under a Chinese Parasol Tree* was created from a piece of white jade with a yellowish-brown crust during the reign of Emperor Qianlong of the Qing Dynasty.

In the jade carving, a moon door divides the yard into two parts. The front side of the carving depicts the scene outside: To the right of the door, a lady stands in the shade of a Chinese parasol tree (*Firmiana simplex*) beside grotesque rocks while holding *ganoderma fungus* (a symbol of good luck in Chinese culture) in her hands. The back side of the carving depicts the scene inside: On the left are banana trees, a stone table, and stone stools, and on the right is another lady gracefully holding a vase. The moon door is semi-closed, with light penetrating through the crack. It seems that the two ladies on both sides of the door were chatting through the opening.

The jade carving is skillfully designed from a piece of jade leftover after making a bowl. The craftsman ingeniously used its original shape and color to create a moon door in the hollowed-out

玉山背面左侧细节

A close-up of the left side on the back of the jade carving.

的艺术杰作。嗜玉成癖的乾隆皇帝，对来之不易的玉料格外珍惜，曾下旨要求制作玉器的余料要加以利用，他也因此对这件玉器情有独钟，作诗一首，刻在玉器的底部。

这件巧夺天工的玉山，向世人完美地诠释了设计与创意的魅力。

玉山正面右侧细节

A close-up of the right side on the front of the jade carving.

center and the tree leaves with its yellowish-brown crust, creating a natural artistic masterpiece.

Emperor Qianlong, who was obsessed with jade, cherished the hard-won jade materials and once decreed that leftover jade materials be recycled for reuse. He loved this piece of jade carving in particular and composed a poem on its bottom.

This jade carving perfectly manifests the charm of ingenious designs.

各种釉彩大瓶

各种釉彩大瓶，清代景德镇御窑厂烧造，瓶高86厘米，口径27厘米。

瓶子从上到下，使用了15种不同的釉彩来装饰。陶瓷加工过程中，不同釉彩的烧制工艺与温度不同。仿汝釉、窑变釉与青花等属高温釉彩，需优先烧制。粉彩、珐琅彩等属低温釉彩，需要后入窑烧制。所以，这件器物需多次入窑出窑，多次烧制，稍有不慎，整器皆毁。其成功制作表明乾隆时期御窑厂已经全面掌握各种釉彩的烧造技艺与性能特点。瓶的腹部有12幅图，6幅为写实图画，绘“丹凤朝阳”“太平有象”“仙山琼阁”等，另外6幅则是吉祥寓意的蝙蝠（与“福”谐音）、如意、灵芝、花卉

瓶底部

The bottom of the vase.

Multi-Glazed Vase

The multi-glazed vase, 86 centimeters in height and 27 centimeters in mouth diameter, was produced by Jingdezhen Imperial Kiln in the Qing Dynasty.

The entire vase features 15 glazes and colors. In porcelain production, different glazes and colors are required to be fired at different temperatures with different techniques.

High-temperature colored glazes such as imitated Ru Kiln glaze, flambé glaze, and blue-and-white glaze need to be fired first in the kiln, and low-temperature colored glazes such as famille-rose glaze and enamel glaze need to be fired later. Therefore, the firing process for this artifact was repeated several times, and any careless move might have ruined the whole piece. Its successful production proved that the imperial kiln in the Qianlong period had fully mastered the firing techniques and characteristics of various glazes.

Twelve images are featured on the belly of the vase, of which six are realistic paintings depicting phoenixes worshiping the morning sun,

瓶颈部

The neck of the vase.

等。图画皆在框内，好像瓶子上的一扇扇开窗，称为“开光”。瓶底有“大清乾隆年制”款识。

各种釉彩大瓶集高温低温、釉上釉下等多种釉彩装饰于一身，因此这件大瓶素有“瓷母”之美称，传世仅此一件，弥足珍贵。它集中体现了当时高超的制瓷技艺，展现了当时顶尖的制作工艺和海纳百川的文化自信，同时也为中国瓷器文化和世界瓷器文化的繁荣与发展做出了巨大贡献。

瓶腹部

The belly of the vase.

elephants, and fairylands, among others, with the other six being decorative patterns of animals, plants, and objects symbolizing auspiciousness such as the bats (homophonic with "福 (*fu*)" in Chinese, meaning "good fortune"), jade Ruyi, *ganoderma fungus*, and flowers.

The images are all framed like windows on the vase, which is known as *Kaiguang* (literally, "open light"). At the bottom of the vase is the mark "Made in Emperor Qianlong's reign of the Qing Dynasty".

The multi-glazed vase features a variety of glazes and colors such as high-temperature and low-temperature glazes, overglaze colors, and underglaze colors, earning the reputation of "mother of porcelain".

As the only of its kind preserved to this day, the precious vase embodies the superb porcelain-making skills of its time and the inclusiveness of Chinese culture, contributing to the development and prosperity of porcelain culture in China and even the world.

金嵌珍珠宝石藏经匣

金嵌珍珠宝石藏经匣，清乾隆年间制作。先以黄金做出形状扁长的匣子，匣体使用宫廷的金嵌珍珠宝石工艺制作，镶嵌上珍珠、红宝石、青金石等，显示出皇家的富贵之气。打开匣盖，内侧彩绘有释迦牟尼佛与二弟子图，色泽鲜艳，细节生动，为宫中画师所绘。

“藏经匣”顾名思义，专用于存放佛经。此件藏经匣中存放着满文《大悲正经》，为梵夹装。“梵夹装”原指古印度把写在贝多罗树叶上的梵文佛经穿绳相连，再用两木板相夹的装帧形式。五代时期，中国已有与此类似的装帧形式出现。到明清时有所演变，书写材料从贝叶变成纸张，但仍保留狭长的形状；页与页之间不再穿洞系绳，而是数页集为一沓，直接用两块木板上下相夹，再用布带捆扎或用匣盒盛装。

这件藏经匣中，经书内容来自印度，用满文书写，反映了清朝包容不同文化信仰的态度。

Gold Sutra Container Inlaid with Pearls and Gemstones

The Gold Sutra Container Inlaid with Pearls and Gemstones dates back to Emperor Qianlong's reign of the Qing Dynasty. First, the craftsman made a rectangular box with gold and then inlaid it with pearls, rubies, lapis lazuli, and other gemstones to demonstrate a sense of imperial dignity. Opening the lid of the box reveals a painting of Sakyamuni and his two disciples, which features bright colors and vivid depiction. The painting was created by a royal painter.

As its name suggests, a sutra container was used to contain Buddhist scriptures. Stored in this sutra container is a Manchu version of *The Great Compassion Sutra* using fold bindings, which originated from the binding method for ancient Indian Buddhist scriptures written in Sanskrit on palm leaves bound with ropes and using two wooden plates as covers. As early as the Five Dynasties period (907-960), books using a similar binding method had appeared in China. During the Ming and Qing dynasties, the method evolved: Palm leaves were replaced by paper, but the elongated and narrow shape was retained. Instead of piercing holes on the pages to tether them together with a rope, several pages were stacked together and directly clamped between two wooden plates, and then tied with cloth tapes or packed in boxes.

The sutra stored in the container, its original text from ancient India, is written in the Manchu language, reflecting the inclusive attitude of the High Qing era towards exotic cultures and beliefs.

田黄三联印

田黄三联印制作于清乾隆时期，包括两枚正方形印和一枚椭圆形印，高度 1 厘米，正方形印边长 2.6 厘米，椭圆形印长径 3 厘米，短径 2.3 厘米，三枚印通过三条活环连接在一起。三枚印章和所有活环链，由一整块田黄石雕刻而成，雕工精绝，显示出制作者的极高造诣。

田黄是中国特有的“软宝石”，材质温润凝腻，居软质雕刻石第一品。以田黄雕刻成的御用玺印及艺术品被尊为“石帝”。乾隆皇帝大量收藏田黄，多用来治印。

两枚正方形印，分别为“乾隆宸翰”和“惟精惟一”，椭圆形印为“乐天”，并饰以螭纹。“惟精惟一”“乐天”出自儒家经典，乾隆借此表明其精心一意的施政思想和乐天知命的人

A Trio of Linked Seals Carved from Tianhuang Stone

The Trio of Linked Seals Carved from Tianhuang Stone, dating back to the reign of Emperor Qianlong of the Qing Dynasty, consists of two square seals and an oval seal, which are linked together by three chains. Each square seal has a side length of 2.6 centimeters, and the oval seal has a major axis of three centimeters and a minor axis of 2.3 centimeters, all with a height of one centimeter. The seals and chains were exquisitely carved from the same piece of Tianhuang stone, testifying to the superb skills of the creator.

Unique to China, Tianhuang stone (mainly consisting of such minerals as dickite and pyrophyllite, among others) is dubbed "soft gemstone" for its jade-like texture. It is the most famous soft stone material used for carving in China. Imperial seals and artworks crafted with this kind of stone are venerated as "kings of stones". Emperor Qianlong collected a large quantity of Tianhuang stone for seal cutting.

The two square seals were engraved with the Chinese characters "乾隆宸翰" (*Qianlong chenhan*, meaning "inscriptions by Emperor Qianlong") and "惟精惟一" (*weijing weiyi*, meaning

生态度。

此印备受乾隆皇帝青睐，常钤盖在其书画上，以后各帝也十分珍视。末代皇帝溥仪被逐出宫时携出此印，且随身不离，至1950年才将其交出，经有关机构移交故宫博物院。

印章和印记，从左到右分别是：“乾隆宸翰”“乐天”“惟精惟一”

The seals and their impressions. From left to right: “乾隆宸翰” (*Qianlong chenhan*, meaning “inscriptions by Emperor Qianlong”), “乐天” (*letian*, meaning “contentment”), and “惟精惟一” (*weijing weiyi*, meaning “purity and dedication”).

“purity and dedication”), and the oval one carries the words “乐天” (*letian*, meaning “contentment”). Both “*weijingweiyi*” and “*letian*” were quoted from Confucian classics. This was how Emperor Qianlong expressed his commitment to state governance and his life philosophy of being content with one’s lot.

Emperor Qianlong was extremely fond of this set of seals and often used them to affix stamps on his calligraphic works and paintings. They were also treasured by later emperors. Puyi, the last emperor of the Qing Dynasty, took the seals with him when he was forced to vacate the palace. Not until 1950 were the seals returned to the Palace Museum via relevant departments.

民安。

金瓯永固杯

金瓯永固杯是清宫举行元旦开笔仪式时专门用来盛放“屠苏酒”的器具。除夕子夜，元旦伊始，皇帝将可祛恶避邪的“屠苏酒”注入杯中，陈于养心殿案上，题写新年吉语，祈愿国泰民安。

夔龙形杯耳

Dragon-shaped cup handle.

Jin'ou Yonggu Cup

The *Jin'ou Yonggu* Cup was used to hold *Tusu* wine during the "pen-opening" ceremony held on Chinese New Year in the Qing Dynasty. When ringing out the old year and ringing in the new year, the emperor poured *Tusu* wine, which was believed to have the power to expel evil, into the cup and placed it on a desk in the Hall of Mental Cultivation. He then wrote good wishes for the coming year, praying for prosperity and peace.

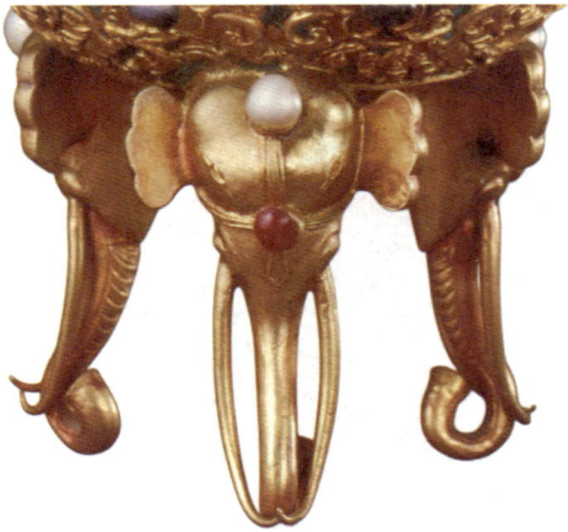

象首式杯足
Elephant head-shaped cup legs.

杯身錾满缠枝宝相花纹，花心以珍珠及红、蓝宝石等镶嵌而成。两侧为夔龙形杯耳，龙头顶珠。杯有三足，呈象首式，头朝下，鼻撑地。杯口一面刻篆书“金瓯永固”，另一面刻“乾隆年制”。制作此杯时，已是嘉庆年间，但退位后的乾隆皇帝以太上皇身份临朝理政，宫内仍沿用乾隆年号，所以此杯上依然署“乾隆”年款。传世的金瓯永固杯共四件，另三件其中一件藏于台北故宫博物院，另外两件藏于伦敦华莱士典藏馆。

金瓯象征国土完整、国家繁荣。“金瓯永固杯”凭借美好的寓意和精巧的造型、华丽的装饰，成为故宫博物院独具皇家特色的瑰宝。

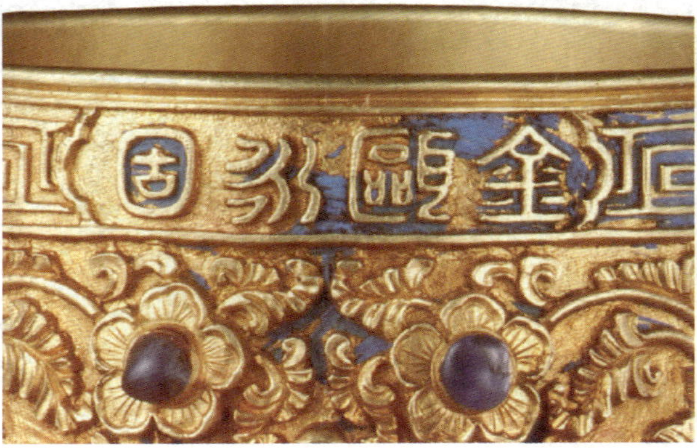

杯口一面刻篆书"金瓯永固"

On one side of the cup mouth is engraved with the seal-script Chinese characters "金瓯永固" (*jin'ou yonggu*, or "the golden goblet remains strong forever").

The cup is adorned with intertwining *baoxiang* flowers, a pattern created based on a combination of lotus and peony, with the flower cores inlaid with pearls, rubies, and sapphires. The cup's handles on both sides are shaped like dragons, each carrying a pearl on its head.

The three legs are designed into downward elephant heads, with curled trunks supporting it on the ground. On one side of the cup mouth is engraved with the seal-script Chinese characters "金瓯永固" (*jin'ou yonggu*, meaning "the golden goblet remains strong forever") and the other side with "乾隆年制" ("Made in Emperor Qianlong's reign").

In fact, the cup was crafted during the reign of Emperor Jiaqing (1796-1820). Given that Qianlong remained in charge of state affairs as a retired emperor after his abdication, the imperial palace still used his reign title. This is why the cup is inscribed with "Made in Emperor Qianlong's reign".

Four such cups have survived to the present day. Of the other three, one is housed in the Palace Museum in Taipei, and the other two in the Wallace Collection in London.

The *Jin'ou Yonggu* Cup symbolizes territorial integrity and national prosperity. With symbolic significance, ingenious design, and gorgeous decorations, it is a unique royal treasure in the collection of the Palace Museum.

青玉、白玉围棋子

玉围棋子分青玉、白玉双色，呈扁圆形，其中青玉棋子 180 枚、白玉棋子 185 枚，质地光洁，做工精良，分别盛放于黑漆描金的棋盒内，盒绘缠枝莲纹。

作为中国古老的棋类游戏之一，围棋对局在春秋时期已较为普遍。早期围棋多为木质，汉时出现了石质围棋，隋代则有瓷质围棋，玉质围棋则最早见于唐代。

唐宋到明清，围棋广泛流行于文人雅士之间，既是一种竞技游戏，也是重要的社交方式。棋盘是双方博弈的“战场”。纵横两组平行线垂直交叉的“阵地”上，对弈者你攻我守，各显神通。一局终了，根据棋子围成的空位与子数相加，多者为胜。对局全程不用言语交流，但凭手执棋子斗智斗勇，因此围棋又得名“手谈”。

随着围棋传入朝鲜半岛、日本等地，越来越多的外国友人接受并认同了围棋。其所蕴含的布局谋篇、包容统一的文化精神，也为世界认知并理解。

Jade Go Chess Pieces

The flat circular Go pieces include 180 made of green jade and 185 made of white jade. With smooth and lustrous appearance and exquisite craftsmanship, they are respectively contained in black lacquer boxes painted with gold and intertwining lotus patterns.

One of the oldest board games in China, Go, commonly known in China as *weiqi*, was already popular as early as the Spring and Autumn Period. In its early days, the game used wooden pieces, and stone pieces emerged during the Han Dynasty, followed by porcelain in the Sui Dynasty and jade in the Tang Dynasty.

From the Tang and Song dynasties to the Ming and Qing times, Go was popular among the literati as both a competitive game and a way of socializing. With a board composed of intersected lines as the "battlefield", the two players "fight" with their wits. To win, the player must use black or white pieces to surround more territory than the opponent. The players don't need verbal communication throughout the game, but use the pieces in their hands to communicate logical strategies. For this reason, Go is also called "hand talk".

With the introduction of Go to the Korean Peninsula, Japan, and other places, the game won recognition from more and more people around the world thanks to the cultural values of big-picture thinking, inclusiveness, and unity it conveys.

紫檀镶金嵌玉箸

紫檀镶金嵌玉箸由紫檀与金、玉搭配制成。紫檀做工极其精致，以金、银丝嵌入，勾勒出奢华的线状花纹。箸身镶嵌金、玉，均为素面不作雕琢，箸端镶嵌莲苞式玉顶，既显金之富丽华美，又有玉之温润典雅。

箸专门用于夹取食物，自古以来，材质各有不同。据记载，商代晚期已有象牙箸。两汉以后，铜、竹、金、玉等均可用于制箸。明代，江苏吴县船家外出时忌讳说“住”，因“箸”和“住”同音，便把“箸”称为“快儿”，意为保佑航船快速到达。随时间推移，“快儿”逐渐被“筷子”取代。清代，箸是新婚庆典的吉祥之物。帝后大婚设合卺宴，婚房内备有两双由红线系在一起的箸，帝后以此共食子孙饽饽（饺子）、长寿面，表达夫妇同心、子孙满堂、健康长寿等美好寓意。

小小一副箸，用材珍贵、工艺精致，既是别出心裁、独具匠心的体现，又是中华文化发展传承的见证。

紫檀镶金嵌玉箸局部

A close-up of the Red Sandalwood Chopsticks Inset with Gold and Jade.

Red Sandalwood Chopsticks Inset with Gold and Jade

This pair of Red Sandalwood Chopsticks Inset with Gold and Jade features exquisite craftsmanship and gorgeous thread-shaped patterns formed by inlaid gold and silver wires. The gold and jade insets on the chopsticks are plain, without any decorative patterns. The jade lotus bud-shaped top showcases both the gorgeousness of gold and the elegance of jade.

Chopsticks are used to pick up food. Since ancient times, a variety of materials have been used to make chopsticks. Historical records show that ivory chopsticks had emerged in the late Shang Dynasty. Materials such as copper, bamboo, gold, and jade were used after the Han Dynasty.

In the Ming Dynasty, saying "*zhu*" (meaning "stop") was taboo among boatmen in Wuxian, today's Jiangsu Province. Because chopsticks were also called "*zhu*" in Chinese, locals began to call them "*kuai*" (meaning "fast") to pray for smooth sailing.

During the Qing Dynasty, chopsticks were used to symbolize blessings at weddings. When the emperor and empress were married, two pairs of chopsticks tied together with red threads would be placed in their wedding room, and they used the chopsticks to eat dumplings and noodles together, a practice conveying good wishes of conjugal felicity, plentiful offspring, health, and longevity.

This pair of chopsticks, featuring precious materials and exquisite craftsmanship, testifies not only to the craftsman's ingenuity, but also to the inheritance and development of Chinese culture.

五

文物交流与文明互鉴

紫禁城的六百年历史中，始终有文明交流的印记。无论是海纳百川的建筑风格，融通内外的制作工艺，还是友好互动的往来人员，都见证了中华文明与世界其他文明的深度对话。时至今日，故宫博物院不仅守护着中华文化遗产及其历史记忆，更肩负着推动文明交流互鉴的重要使命，通过国际展览、学术交流、人员培训等多种形式，在世界舞台上以故宫文化魅力，推动落实全球文明倡议，书写人类文明交流互鉴的新篇章。

INTERNATIONAL EXCHANGE ON CULTURAL HERITAGE AND MUTUAL LEARNING AMONG CIVILIZATIONS

Cultural exchange has penetrated the 600-year history of the Forbidden City. Its inclusive architectural style, production techniques integrating Chinese and foreign elements, and personnel exchange with its overseas counterparts all testify to the in-depth dialogue between Chinese and other civilizations.

Today, the Palace Museum not only serves as a guardian for Chinese cultural heritage and its historical memory, but also shoulders the important mission of promoting exchange and mutual learning among civilizations.

Through international exhibitions, academic exchanges, personnel training and other channels, the museum has been committed to advancing the implementation of the Global Civilization Initiative on the world stage with its cultural charm, and writing a new chapter of exchange and mutual learning among human civilizations.

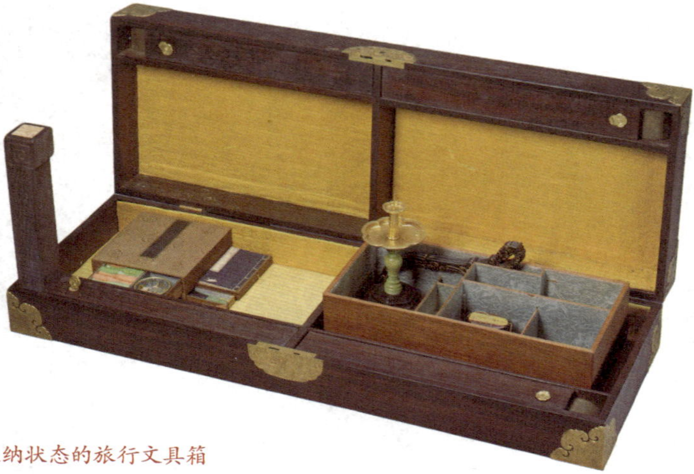

收纳状态的旅行文具箱

Stationery case used as a container.

旅行文具箱

旅行文具箱为中国清朝乾隆时期制作，用于乾隆皇帝出行时处理政务和读书。此文具箱设计精巧，四条桌腿放在箱槽中时，它是一个可收纳的箱子，按动机关，拉出桌腿固定好，再翻转木箱，就变成高 40 厘米的书桌，很适合喜爱旅行的乾隆皇帝。箱内有两个屉盒，盒内是多宝格，可放置小巧精细的文具，如白玉洗、松花江石砚、石章、描金云龙纹笔、银制成套绘图器等，共 64 件 / 套，均是乾隆皇帝喜用的文房佳品。

2008 年，故宫博物院和法国卢浮宫博物馆联合举办“卢浮宫·拿破仑一世展”，拿破仑的旅行用品箱第一次来到故宫。这是以桃花心木制成的长方形箱子，存放的旅行用品多达 92 件，其中 78 件是梳洗用品。箱盖里也暗藏着一个机关，按动后出现一面镜子，供箱主人梳妆打扮之用。

两个旅行箱有异曲同工之妙，不仅体现出中西不同文化之间鲜明个性，也有相通的共性，皆凝结了人们对智慧和美的思考与实践。

变成书桌的旅行文具箱

Stationery case used as a desk.

Stationary Case

The stationery case was made during the reign of Emperor Qianlong of the Qing Dynasty for the convenience of the emperor to read and handle government affairs while he was traveling.

This stationery case was ingeniously designed. When the four legs were placed in the slots, it served as a box to store stationery. When a mechanical device was pressed, the four legs could be dragged out, and the wooden case was placed adversely, transforming it into a 40-centimeter-tall desk. It was suitable for Emperor Qianlong, who loved traveling.

The case has two drawers with grids used to hold the emperor's diverse delicate stationery such as white jade brush washers, Songhua inkstones, stone seals, gold-lacquered brush pens with dragon patterns, and silver drawing apparatus sets, 64 pieces/sets in total. All of them were favorite stationery of Emperor Qianlong.

In 2008, the Palace Museum and the Louvre in France jointly organized the Napoleon I exhibition, and a suitcase used by Napoleon was exhibited at the Palace Museum for the first time. It is a rectangular case made of mahogany that stored up to 92 travel items, 78 of which were toiletries. It also has a hidden mechanical device, and when pressed, a mirror would pop out for makeup.

The two cases for traveling are both ingenious. They not only reflect the differences and commonalities between Chinese and Western cultures, but also condense everyday wisdom and aesthetics.

《雍正洋装像》

《雍正洋装像》为半身像，画面为纸本设色，使用木框玻璃屏装裱。

雍正皇帝是中国清朝第五位皇帝，入关定都北京后的第三位皇帝。雍正皇帝在位期间，对内改革清廷的机构和吏制，对外平定边疆叛乱，打下了良好的政治和经济基础。他还酷爱扮装，常命画师将自己的各种形象描绘入画，如道士、农夫、喇嘛、猎手等。这幅画像中，他头戴烫成小卷的假发，颈部系淡蓝领巾，着深绿外衣。此画使用中国画矿物颜料，风格却受西洋画写实手法影响，尤其衣服的花纹细节，甚至六颗纽扣，都清晰而且精致，甚至雍正皇帝下巴上的痣也描绘得细致入微。

雍正皇帝在位的同时期为法王路易十五执政，中法贸易与文化交流依然频繁。这幅身着欧式服装的中国皇帝像，是17—18世纪中法两国交流往来的缩影，见证了这一时期东西方文明的交流互鉴。

服饰细节

A close-up of the clothing Emperor Yongzheng wears in the portrait.

头像细节

A close-up of Emperor Yongzheng's head in the portrait.

A Portrait of Emperor Yongzheng in Western Suit

This half-length portrait of Emperor Yongzheng in a Western suit, color on paper, was mounted with a wooden frame and glass.

Yongzheng was the fifth emperor of the Qing Dynasty and the third after the Qing empire moved its capital to Beijing. During his reign, Emperor Yongzheng reformed the government institutions and bureaucratic system and quelled rebellions in the frontiers, laying a sound foundation for political and economic development. He loved cosplay and often ordered court painters to depict his portraits as various identities, such as a Taoist, farmer, lama, and hunter, among others.

In this portrait, he wears a wig permed into small curls, a pale-blue scarf around his neck, and a dark-green coat. The portrait features mineral pigments of traditional Chinese painting, but its style was influenced by the realistic techniques of Western painting. In particular, the detailed patterns of the clothes including the six buttons were vividly depicted, and even the mole on the emperor's chin was clearly portrayed.

The reign of Emperor Yongzheng roughly corresponded with that of King Louis XV of France. Back then, China and France engaged in frequent trade and cultural exchange. This portrait of a Chinese emperor dressed in European-style costume epitomizes the interactions between China and France in the 17th and 18th centuries, testifying to the exchange and mutual learning between Eastern and Western civilizations at the time.

银镀金浑天仪

在中国历代帝王中，康熙是系统认真学习过西方天文、地理、数学、医药等各种学科的帝王，而且还主持推动了多项大规模的科学活动，对中西科技文化交流做出了巨大贡献。

银镀金浑天仪是康熙皇帝学习天文知识时所用的教具，象征着清代贵族阶层对外来文化的接纳与融合。仪器被放置在紫檀木底座中，有三层银镀金圈环，外层是地平圈、子午圈、赤

Gilded Silver Armillary Sphere

Among Chinese emperors of all dynasties, Kangxi was remembered for his commitment to systematically studying Western knowledge of various disciplines such as astronomy, geography, mathematics, and medicine. He also led and promoted many large-scale scientific activities, making great contributions to the Sino-European exchange in science, technology, and culture.

The gilded silver armillary sphere was a teaching instrument used by Emperor Kangxi to study astronomy, indicating that Qing-dynasty nobles began to accept and absorb exotic cultures.

The instrument on a red sandalwood base consists of three sets of rings, one inside another. Those on the outside are the horizontal,

银镀金浑天仪局部

A fragment of the gilded silver armillary sphere.

道圈，圈上刻字显示康熙八年（1669）南怀仁制作。南怀仁是比利时人，曾为清代宫廷服务 28 年，负责天文观测、制定历法、改良武器、设计机械等工作，还担任过康熙皇帝的科学教师。

银镀金浑天仪最中间为地球，地球上还标注了亚洲、欧洲、美洲等大洲当时的名称。仪器可以演示日食与月食现象，表现太阳、月亮围绕地球转动的情景，说明这是一件以地心说为基础的天文演示仪器。对于刚刚结束新旧历法之争的康熙朝，其在再度应用西洋历法、改进中国测天仪器等方面，都起了积极的作用。

meridian, and celestial equator rings.

The inscriptions on the rings indicate that it was made by Ferdinand Verbiest in 1669, the eighth year of the Kangxi reign. A missionary from Belgium, Verbiest served the Qing royal court for 28 years, taking responsibility for work like astronomical observation, calendar formulation, weapon improvement, and machine design. He also acted as a science teacher for Emperor Kangxi.

The innermost ring set of the armillary sphere stands for the earth, which carries the names of continents such as Asia, Europe, and Americas. The instrument can imitate solar and lunar eclipses and show a scene of the sun and moon revolving around the earth, indicating that it is an astronomical instrument based on geocentrism.

Back then, the Kangxi reign had just witnessed a debate between old and new calendars. The emergence of the instrument played a positive role in re-application of the Western calendar and improvements of astrological instruments in China.

绿色玻璃渣斗

渣斗是宫中生活用品，以瓷制、铜制和珐琅制居多，玻璃制的渣斗十分少见。这件绿色玻璃渣斗，喇叭状开口，鼓腹，平底，通体布满六边形花纹，据说是磨制出的图案。高仅有 8.7 厘米，口径 7.7 厘米，大小与苹果相当，十分轻盈，是中国乾隆朝的玻璃精品。

如今，玻璃很是常见，历史上却曾经珍稀昂贵。中国的玻璃历史可以追溯到 2500 年前，曾被称为“琉璃”“料器”。清初开海禁，欧洲玻璃制品进入中国，为皇帝服务的西洋人也把玻璃制作工艺带入宫廷。康熙皇帝专门设立玻璃厂，隶属于养心殿造办处，为宫中生产各种玻璃制品，“玻璃”之称也正式确立。

古代中国最初将玻璃器视为人造玉石，推崇不透明的玻璃器。欧洲则喜好像水晶一样的透明玻璃，这一喜好影响了后来清宫玻璃器的制作。以这件绿色渣斗为代表，清宫玻璃厂生产的高透明度玻璃器，正是中西方技艺与审美相互融合的产物。

Green Glass Cuspidor

As living utensils in the imperial palace, cuspidors were mostly made of porcelain, brass or enamel, and glass pieces were very rare.

A glass masterpiece dating back to the reign of Emperor Qianlong of the Qing Dynasty, this green glass cuspidor features a trumpet-shaped mouth, a plump belly and a flat bottom. Its body is decorated with hexagonal patterns that are believed to be ground manually. The cuspidor measures 8.7 centimeters tall and 7.7 centimeters in mouth diameter, the size of an apple, and looks exquisite and light.

Glass is common today, but in the past it was rare and expensive. The history of glassmaking in China can be traced back to 2,500 years ago, and glass was once called "*liuli*" or "*liaoqi*" in Chinese.

After restrictions on maritime trade were lifted in the Qing Dynasty, European glassware entered China, and Westerners who served the emperor also brought glassmaking technology into the royal court. Emperor Kangxi set up a glass factory under the Imperial Workshop in the Hall of Mental Cultivation to produce various glass products for the palace. From then on, glass began to be formally called "*boli*" in Chinese.

Initially, the ancient Chinese regarded glassware as artificial jade and admired opaque glassware. In contrast, Europeans preferred crystal-like transparent glass. This preference influenced glassware production in the Qing royal court. The glass factory in the Qing imperial palace was committed to producing high-transparency glassware that fused Chinese and Western techniques and aesthetics. This green glass cuspidor is representative of that trend.

自来火鸟枪

这是一把西洋自来火鸟枪。射击时通过簧轮、燧石碰撞起火，引燃膛内火药发射子弹。枪管铁质，装有木托，绘西洋花蔓草纹，浮雕盾、刀、斧等图案。枪管后部上方嵌木质军人半身像，人像的帽钉、腰带、扣袢用黄金装饰。枪管上用英文标注有枪的制造者和制作地点等信息。枪上系皮质条签，以满、汉、蒙、藏四种文字分别书写“乾隆五十八年八月英咕唎国王热沃尔日恭进自来火鸟枪一杆”。

1793 年，马戛尔尼使团携英王乔治三世致乾隆皇帝的国书和西洋礼物来华，在避暑山庄获得中国乾隆皇帝接见，这是英国政府派出的第一个正式访华使团，而这件自来火鸟枪便是进献给乾隆皇帝的国礼之一。由于文化差异，中英两方对于使者

Fowling Piece

This gun is a European fowling piece. When firing, the wheellock and the flint collide to ignite the gunpowder in the firing chamber to shoot the bullet. The fowling piece features an iron gun barrel equipped with a wooden support painted with arabesque patterns and embossed with shields, knives, axes and other motifs.

A wooden bust of a soldier is embedded above the rear of the barrel, with cap nails, belt, and buckle loop decorated with gold. The barrel is marked with information in English such as the gun's maker and production location.

The gun is tied with a leather label, carrying words in Manchu, Han, Mongolian and Tibetan scripts, translated as "a fowling piece presented by King George III of England as a gift to his majesty in the eighth month of the 58th year of Emperor Qianlong's reign".

In 1793, a mission led by Earl George Macartney visited China, with a letter and gifts from King George III to Emperor Qianlong.

As the first official diplomatic delegation sent by the British government to China, they were received by Emperor Qianlong at Chengde Mountain Resort. This fowling piece was one of the state

枪管后部上方

Upper back of the barrel of the fowling piece.

是否跪拜皇帝一事各执己见。最终，马戛尔尼以单膝跪地的方式，觐见了乾隆皇帝。

古代中国火药发明与近代西方枪械制造融合产生的自来火鸟枪，成为东西方科技文化交流的有力见证。

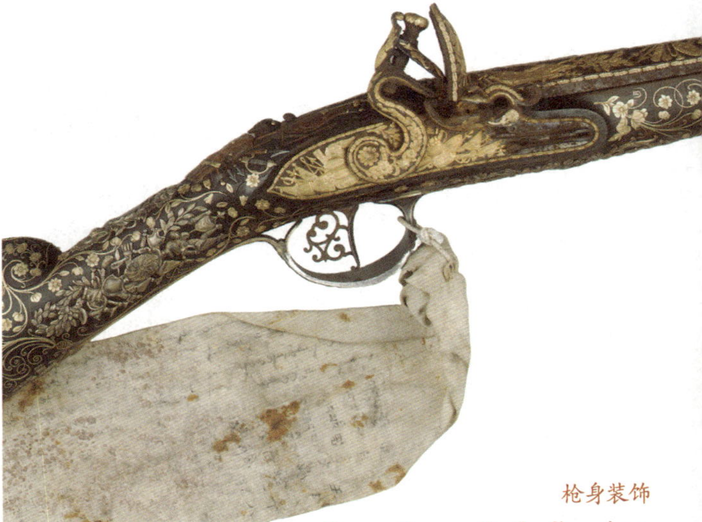

枪身装饰

Decorations on the fowling piece.

gifts presented to Emperor Qianlong. Due to cultural clashes, the two sides had disagreements on whether the British envoys should kneel to the Chinese emperor. In the end, Macartney knelt on one knee when being granted an audience with Emperor Qianlong.

A combination of gunpowder invented in ancient China and modern firearm manufacturing technology of the West, the fowling piece speaks volumes for East-West exchanges in science, technology and culture.

铜镀金写字人钟

机械钟表自明代万历时期进入北京紫禁城，继而成为重要的宫廷陈设、收藏。如今故宫博物院仍藏有中外钟表1500余件，铜镀金写字人钟便是个中精品。

写字人钟为铜镀金四层楼阁。顶层圆亭内两铜人举横幅站立，机械启动时，两人手举横幅缓缓展开，上书“万寿无疆”四字。圆亭下的楼阁上有一敲钟人，位于表盘正上方，每逢3、6、9、12时报时完毕，便会击打钟碗奏乐。表盘为第三层。下面一层为底层，是此钟最精彩、新奇的部分：写字机械人。

Gilded Copper Clock with a Writing Figure

Mechanical clocks were introduced to the Forbidden City in Beijing during the reign of Emperor Wanli of the Ming Dynasty and quickly became important ornaments in the royal collection. Today, the Palace Museum houses more than 1,500 pieces of vintage clocks from both home and abroad, and this gilded copper clock with a writing figure is a standout among them.

The clock is shaped like a four-story pavilion. Two copper figures stand in the round pavilion on the top. When the mechanical system starts, a banner held by the two figures unfolds slowly, displaying four Chinese characters "万寿无疆", meaning "boundless longevity".

On the floor beneath the round pavilion is a bell ringer directly above the dial, who strikes a bowl-shaped bell to play music after the announcement of 3, 6, 9, or 12 o'clock. The dial is on the second floor. The first floor is the most spectacular and ingenious part—a mechanical figure who can write.

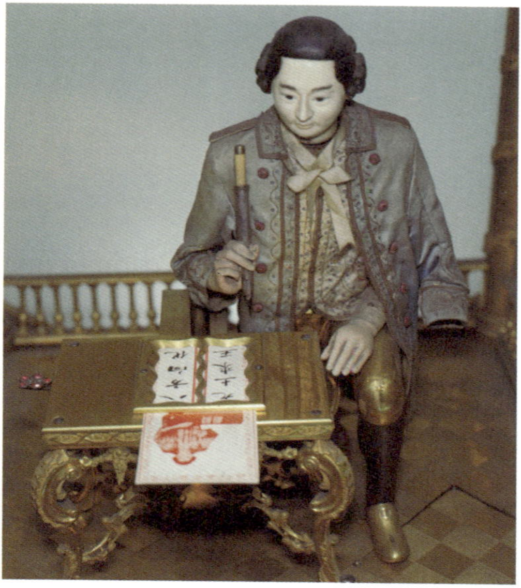

钟表底层的机械写字人

The writing figure on the first floor of the clock in the shape of a four-story pavilion.

写字人为欧洲绅士模样，单膝跪地，右手执毛笔，上弦后可在面前纸条上写出“八方向化，九土来王”8个汉字，头部也会随之摆动。而这一切完全通过机芯内庞杂精密的机械结构控制完成，可谓是机械艺术之杰作。

此钟为18世纪英国著名的制钟世家威廉森专为清宫制造，做工精湛，机械表演复杂多样，颇受乾隆皇帝喜爱，是中西文化融合在钟表上的最佳体现。

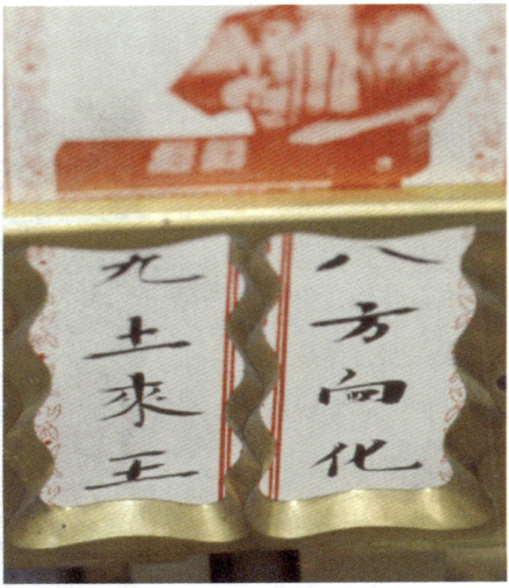

机械写字人书写的“八方向化，九土来王”纸条

The eight Chinese characters “八方向化，九土来王”, translated as “All from eight directions and nine territories bow down to his majesty”, written by the mechanical figure on the clock.

The writing figure is a European gentleman, who kneels on one knee while holding a brush pen in his right hand. After winding, he will write eight Chinese characters, “八方向化，九土来王”, translated as “All from eight directions and nine territories bow down to his majesty”, and his head will swing accordingly. All of this is controlled entirely by the intricate mechanical structure of the clock movement, making it a masterpiece of mechanical art.

This clock was made for the Qing royal court by Williamson, a famous British clockmaker family in the 18th Century. With exquisite craftsmanship and intricate mechanical designs, it was loved by Emperor Qianlong very much. The clock perfectly embodies integration of Chinese and Western cultures in clockmaking.

紫檀楼阁更钟

紫檀楼阁更钟制作于中国清乾隆年间，白天走时、报时，晚上打更。

整体以紫檀木为框架，辅以珐琅、玉石装饰，集多种制作技艺于一身，体现了清宫造办处钟表的典型特征。钟上部为重檐楼阁，中部铜镀金面板上錾刻莲花，上嵌表盘、节气盘、定更盘。下部为须弥座。表盘最大，用于走时，与一般西洋钟表无异。两小盘分别是节气盘与定更盘，用于打更。打更是中国传统的夜间报时方法。古人将夜晚时长等分为五段，即五更，每更报时。由于不同节气的起更时间、更间长短不同，便需要由节气盘和定更盘来调节更的起讫和间隔时间，保证夜间准确打更。制作难度比一般时钟更大。

Red Sandalwood Pavilion-Shaped Clock

The Red Sandalwood Pavilion-shaped Clock, dating back to the Qing Emperor Qianlong's reign, was used to both announce time in the daytime and sound the night watches.

With red sandalwood as the main framework, the clock is embellished with enamel and gemstones and involves a wide range of techniques, demonstrating a typical style of the Imperial Workshop of the Qing Dynasty.

The upper part of the clock is a double-eave pavilion, and the gilded copper facade is engraved with lotus flower patterns and inlaid with a big dial as well as two smaller meters indicating solar terms and night watches, respectively. The bottom is a Buddhist-style Xumi base.

The ancient Chinese divided the night into five *geng*s equivalent to two hours each, and stroke gongs to announce the time at the turn of each *geng*, which is called "*dageng*" (meaning "sound the night watches"). Since the start and end time and length of each *geng* vary in different solar terms, the two smaller meters were necessary to accurately sound the night watches. This design made the clock more difficult to make than a regular one.

节气盘与定更盘

The two smaller meters indicate solar terms and night watches, respectively.

西洋钟表于 17 世纪初叶由西方传教士带入宫廷，雍正皇帝不满足于单纯使用西方计时方式，要求工匠在西洋人的帮助下，发明独特的更钟。紫檀楼阁更钟是西方钟表计时与中国传统夜间计时方式的融合，是中西方科技、文化交流碰撞出的创新成果。

European clocks were brought into the Qing royal court by Western missionaries in the early 17th Century. Emperor Yongzheng was not satisfied with simply using Western timekeeping methods, and asked Chinese craftsmen to invent unique clocks with the help of Westerners. This red sandalwood clock fused Western clock timekeeping and traditional Chinese night timekeeping, representing an innovative result of technological and cultural exchanges between China and the West.

画珐琅海棠式花篮

画珐琅海棠式花篮，铜胎，为四瓣海棠式，提梁上饰花卉纹。篮身外侧以黄色珐琅釉为底，绘盛开的粉色大朵牡丹，间或饰蓝色、藕荷色小荷花，寓意“祥和富贵”。篮内侧施天蓝色釉，篮底施白釉，有“康熙御制”款识。

画珐琅技法源于法国，主要使用在铜胎器物上，在康熙早期由粤海关进入中国，在康熙晚期进入宫廷。当时宫廷画珐琅器烧造技术不高，还特请欧洲及广州画珐琅匠师参与指导。乾隆皇帝还曾将此花篮作为范式，要求照样仿制。有的器物画样被送到法国制作，也有的在粤海关完成仿制。如今，法国和粤海关仿制的同款花篮，故宫博物院都有收藏。

清代宫廷自接触画珐琅后，逐渐掌握制造技术并不断精进，还将画珐琅技术运用在陶瓷、玻璃等器物表面，体现了中国自古以来的融合创新能力。

Painted Enamel Begonia Flower Basket

款识

The mark "Made upon the decree of Emperor Kangxi" on the bottom of the enamel flower basket.

The Painted Enamel Begonia Flower Basket, made of copper, is shaped like a four-petal begonia flower. Its handle is embellished with flower patterns. The outside of the basket features yellow enamel glaze, painted with blooming pink peonies and dotted with blue or pinkish-purple lotus flowers, which symbolize "peace and dignity". The inside is coated with azure glaze, and the bottom adopts white glaze and carries the mark "Made upon the decree of Emperor Kangxi".

Painted enameling is a technique originating in France and mainly used on copper objects. It was introduced to China via Guangzhou Customs in the early days of Emperor Kangxi's reign, and then to the royal court in the late Kangxi era. Then, the royal court's firing technology of painted enamel wares remained imperfect, so experienced craftsmen from Europe and Guangzhou were invited to give instructions.

Emperor Qianlong asked craftsmen to make imitations of this flower basket. The blueprints of some objects were sent to France for production, and some imitations were manufactured at Guangzhou Customs. Today, artifacts modeled after this flower basket by craftsmen in France and Guangzhou Customs can be found in the collection of the Palace Museum.

After painted enameling was introduced to the Qing imperial palace, court craftsmen gradually grasped and improved the technique, which they used on the surface of porcelain, glass, and other objects.

白玉错金嵌宝石碗

白玉错金嵌宝石碗，碗口直径约 14 厘米，装饰有桃形双耳、花瓣式圈足，碗壁薄可透光。壁外侧有花叶纹，其中花瓣、花蕊是用 108 颗精雕细琢的红宝石做成，枝叶则是金片组成。壁内侧阴刻楷书乾隆皇帝御制诗一首，共 60 字，说明了此碗的来历、材质和用途。碗内底部正中有隶书“乾隆御用”四字。此碗自乾隆五十一年（1786）制成后始终为乾隆皇帝所珍爱，甚至在庆典活动时还被当作御殿赐茶的用具。

黄金、红宝石组成的完整花叶纹

The branch, leaf, and flower patterns made of gold and rubies.

White Jade Bowl Inlaid with Gold and Gemstones

The White Jade Bowl Inlaid with Gold and Gemstones measures about 14 centimeters in mouth diameter and features two peach-shaped ears, a petal-shaped bottom, and thin and translucent walls.

The outer side of the wall is adorned with the patterns of flowers and leaves. The petals and stamens of the flowers are made of 108 finely carved rubies, and the branches and leaves are crafted with gold sheets. The inside wall is engraved with a 60-word poem by Emperor Qianlong, which explains the origin, material, and usage of this bowl.

At the bottom of the bowl are four Chinese characters "乾隆御用" in *lishu*, or the clerical script, translated as "For the use of Emperor Qianlong". This bowl had been much cherished by Emperor Qianlong since it was made in 1786. It was even used to award tea to ministers by the emperor during important celebrations.

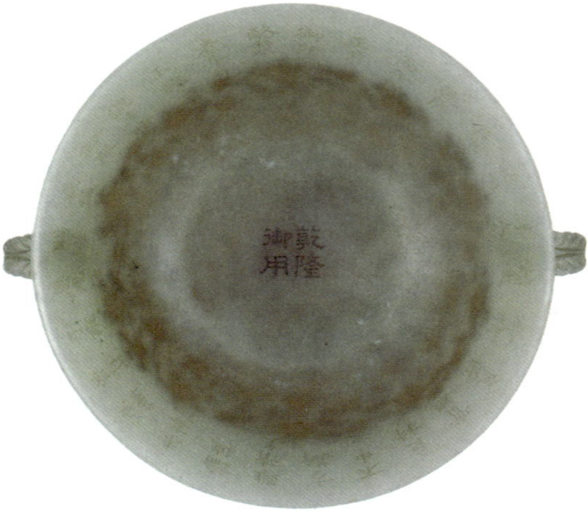

碗内底部“乾隆御用”款识

The mark “For the use of Emperor Qianlong” on the bottom of the bowl.

此碗充满异域文化特色，有典型的痕都斯坦风格。痕都斯坦玉器来自西亚、中亚地区，特征为器物轻薄、多艳丽的镶嵌、刻异域风格花纹，整体纤巧秀美、晶莹剔透。这类玉器在宫廷档案中被称为“西番作”，意即西域特色的作品。

该碗是由清宫造办处制作完成，其高超的玉雕和金银宝石镶嵌技术，呈现了西域的装饰风格，是18世纪中外文化交流融合的例证。

碗壁由红宝石、金片组成的花叶纹局部

The patterns of flowers and leaves made of rubies and gold sheets on the exterior wall of the bowl.

This bowl radiates exotic Hindustan style. Originating from West and Central Asia, Hindustan jade wares are characterized by lightness, gaudy inlays, and exotic carvings, which look exquisite and crystal clear. In the palace archives, such jade objects were called "*xifanzuo*", meaning "works in the style of the Western Regions".

The jade bowl was made by the Imperial Workshop of the Qing Dynasty. Its superb carving and inlaying techniques manifest the decorative style of the Western Regions, evidencing cultural exchange and integration between China and other countries in the 18th Century.

铜镀金香水瓶架

铜镀金香水瓶架为晚清时期舶来品，装有三扇蓝玻璃小门，以弧形铜镀金挂钩作为开关，玻璃门内放置蓝玻璃香水瓶。玻璃门及香水瓶局部装饰彩色贴花及彩绘花。瓶架上方装有铜镀金挂环，便于携带、固定。瓶架底部装有铜镀金支腿，造型极具西方风格。蓝玻璃精致典雅，与镀金形成色彩反差，彰显雍容华贵的宫廷气息。

外国香水制作工艺历史悠久，品质优良，深受清代宫廷女性的青睐。区别于中国本土生产的香粉、香油，外国香水被称为“洋货”，获取渠道主要为各地上贡，或朝廷对外贸易采购，以满足宫廷日用。

精美的装饰与设计，使得香水瓶架本身就是一件艺术品，反映出西方玻璃制作工艺与商品包装设计的时尚典雅。

蓝色玻璃小门

Perfume bottle holder with three small blue glass openings

Gilded Copper Perfume Bottle Holder

The Gilded Copper Perfume Bottle Holder was imported to China during the late Qing Dynasty. It has three small blue glass openings, each with a curved gilded copper hook as a switch, with a blue glass perfume bottle placed inside.

The glass openings and perfume bottle are partially adorned with colorful appliqués and painted flowers. The perfume bottle holder is equipped with a gilded copper ring, making it easy to carry or hang. Its bottom has three gilded copper legs.

The design is in Western style, with the delicate, elegant blue glass in distinct contrast with the gold plating, displaying a graceful and luxurious royal appeal.

Due to its longstanding history and excellent quality, imported perfume was popular among noblewomen in the Qing Dynasty. Imported perfumes were called "foreign goods", to be distinguished from Chinese-made face powder and grease. Back then, the royal court acquired such perfume either by tributes from local officials or through foreign trade.

The exquisite decorations and designs make this perfume bottle holder a real work of art, reflecting the fashionable and elegant style of Western glassmaking and product packaging.

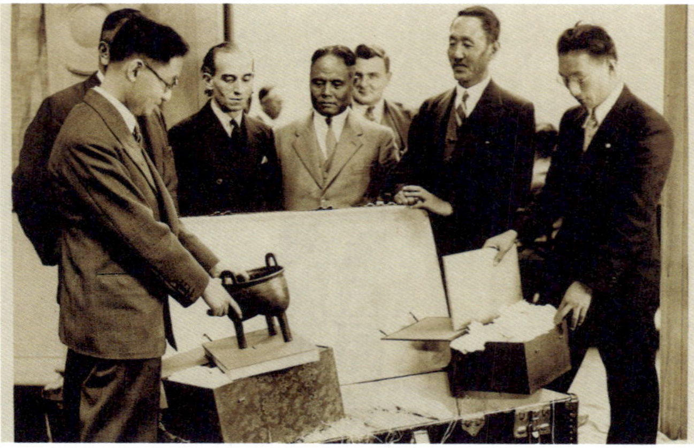

1935 年在伦敦皇家艺术学院举行的开箱仪式
The unpacking ceremony of Palace Museum relics sent to the Royal Academy of Arts in Britain for an exhibition in 1935.

赴英交流展

故宫博物院与英国文博机构长期保持友好合作，数次赴英国举办展览。其中，2005 年与英国皇家艺术学院联合举办的“盛世华章”展最受瞩目，是 1949 年以来故宫博物院展出规模最大、珍品级别最高的赴外展览。

该展览精选中国清代康熙、雍正、乾隆时期约 400 件珍品，涵盖书画、玉器、青铜器、瓷器、漆器、织绣、家具、西洋仪器等类别，95% 来自故宫博物院，其中不少是首次亮相海外。展览生动展现了三位清代皇帝的生平伟业与文化修养，再现了这一时期政治、宗教、军事、文化、艺术的辉煌盛况。早在 1935 年，故宫博物院就曾选送 700 余件文物参加伦敦中国艺术国际博览会，而展厅就设在英国皇家艺术学院。当时博览会吸引了来自德国、意大利、法国等国 40 余万观众，是中华文化走向世界的重要里程碑。

2024 年，故宫博物院与英国科学博物馆合作举办“凝时聚珍”展，首次在英国展出 23 件故宫钟表，成为中英文化交流的又一亮点。

Palace Museum Exhibitions in Britain

The Palace Museum has maintained long-term friendly cooperation with many British museums and cultural institutions. It has sent exhibitions to the UK several times. Among them, *China: The Three Emperors, 1662-1795*, an exhibition co-hosted by the Palace Museum and the Royal Academy of Arts in 2005, drew the greatest attention as the largest and highest-level overseas exhibition of treasures in the Palace Museum since 1949.

The exhibition featured about 400 pieces of treasures from the reigns of Emperors Kangxi, Yongzheng, and Qianlong of the Qing Dynasty, ranging from calligraphy and painting to jade, bronze, porcelain, lacquerware, embroidery, furniture, and Western instruments. Of these relics, 95 percent were from the Palace Museum, and many had never before been exhibited abroad. The exhibition vividly displayed the lives and cultural achievements of the three Qing emperors, reflecting the political, religious, military, cultural, and artistic prosperity of this period.

As early as 1935, the Palace Museum selected more than 700 pieces of relics to participate in the International Exhibition of Chinese Art in London, which was organized by the Royal Academy of Arts. Back then, the exhibition attracted more than 400,000 visitors from Germany, Italy, France, and other countries, marking an important milestone for Chinese culture going global.

In 2024, the Palace Museum joined hands with the Science Museum of Britain to hold the exhibition *Zimingzhong: Clockwork Treasures from China's Forbidden City*, which displayed 23 clocks from the Palace Museum in the UK for the first time, becoming another highlight of China-UK cultural exchange.

“历史之遇”展厅

A view of the *Historic Encounters* exhibition.

午门三联展

2024 年 1 月，故宫博物院在午门同期推出“埃尔奥拉——阿拉伯半岛的奇迹绿洲”“历史之遇——中国与西亚古代文明交流展”和“璀璨波斯——伊朗文物精华展”三大展览。

三大展览各具特色，经“历史之遇”展串联，勾勒出丝绸之路上重要文明的历史长卷。“历史之遇”展，以故宫博物院文物为基础，汇集伊朗国家博物馆等 10 家国内外考古文博机构 266 件（组）文物，讲述中国与西亚相遇相知、交往交流的历史故事。“璀璨波斯”展，汇集伊朗多家博物馆 216 件文物，多是

"璀璨波斯"展厅

A view of *The Glory of Ancient Persia* exhibition.

Three Joint Exhibitions at Meridian Gate

In January 2024, the Palace Museum launched three major exhibitions at the Meridian Gate Exhibition Hall, namely *Al-Ula, Wonder of Arabia*, *Historic Encounters: Interaction Between China and West Asia in History*, and *The Glory of Ancient Persia*.

The three distinctive exhibitions recount the glorious history of major civilizations along the Silk Road.

Based on relics from the Palace Museum, the *Historic Encounters* brings together 266 pieces (sets) of relics from 10 domestic and foreign archaeological and cultural institutions, including the National Museum of Iran, to tell a story of historical interaction and exchange between China and West Asia.

The Glory of Ancient Persia features 216 pieces of relics from various museums in Iran, most of which represent vivid evidence of the long-standing friendship between China and Iran.

The *Al-Ula* exhibition employed sound and light technology to

展览海报
Exhibition posters.

两国友好往来源远流长的鲜活实证。“埃尔奥拉”展，用声光技术呈现沙特西北部城市艾尔奥拉壮丽的沙漠绿洲景观，用230余件（组）文物展示7000年来人类在此繁衍生息的文明奇迹。

此次联展，是故宫博物院践行习近平提出“全球文明倡议”的重要举措，通过回顾中国与西亚古代文明交流互鉴的历史，增进各国人民之间的相互了解，探寻丝绸之路上交流互鉴的文明发展之路。

“埃尔奥拉”展厅

A view of the *Al-Ula* exhibition.

recreate the magnificent oasis landscape of the northwestern Saudi Arabian city of al-Ula. It also features more than 230 pieces (sets) of relics that testify to the miraculous civilization created by local people over the past 7,000 years.

The joint exhibitions were an important move taken by the Palace Museum to implement the Global Civilization Initiative proposed by Chinese President Xi Jinping, which aims to enhance mutual understanding between the peoples of various countries and explore the development of civilizations along the Silk Road by reviewing the history of exchanges and mutual learning between the ancient civilizations of China and West Asia.

"紫禁城与凡尔赛宫"展厅中的康熙皇帝画像

A portrait of Emperor Kangxi displayed at *The Forbidden City and the Palace of Versailles* exhibition.

"紫禁城与凡尔赛宫"展览

2024 年是中法建交 60 周年暨中法文化旅游年。2024 年 4 月 1 日至 6 月 30 日，由故宫博物院和凡尔赛宫殿、博物馆及国家园林公共机构（凡尔赛宫）联合主办的"紫禁城与凡尔赛宫——17、18 世纪的中法交往"展览，在故宫博物院文华殿展厅对公众开放。

该展览精选故宫博物院、凡尔赛宫等多家机构 200 余件藏品，通过"龙与百合花的相遇""紫禁城中的法国风景""凡尔赛宫的中国时尚"三个单元，生动描绘 17、18 世纪中法交往的盛况。1688 年，法国国王路易十四和中国康熙皇帝彼此之间充满浓厚兴趣，因此，五位"国王数学家"到北京，得到康熙

Exhibition: *The Forbidden City and the Palace of Versailles*

展览海报图

Exhibition poster.

The year 2024 was the China-France Year of Culture and Tourism, also marking the 60th anniversary of the establishment of China-France diplomatic ties. From April 1 to June 30, *The Forbidden City and the Palace of Versailles: Exchanges Between China and France in the 17th and 18th Centuries* was held at the Hall of Literary Glory in the Palace Museum. The exhibition was jointly hosted by the Palace Museum and the Palace of Versailles.

The exhibition features 200-plus pieces of relics from a number of institutions including the Palace Museum and the Palace of Versailles and consists of three sections: Encounter of the Dragon and the Fleur-de-lis, The French Landscape in the Forbidden City, and Chinese Vogue at Versailles. It vividly showcased the interactions and exchanges between China and France in the 17th and 18th centuries.

Emperor Kangxi and King Louis XIV of France showed strong interest in each other's country. In 1688, King Louis XIV dispatched some mathematicians to Beijing, who were received by

皇帝接见，其中白晋（Joachim Bouvet）和张诚（Jean-Francois Gerbillon）留在宫廷。此后百余年，两国在政治、经济、科技、文化、艺术等领域展开全方位交流。

紫禁城和凡尔赛宫，是历史上中法交往的见证地，也是各自国家文化的象征符号，在当代延续着交流互鉴的故事。凡尔赛宫和故宫博物院先后合作举办过康熙大帝展、太阳王路易十四展。此次展览开幕也是故宫博物院与法国文化机构交流合作的新开端。

"紫禁城与凡尔赛宫"展厅中的路易十四国王画像

A portrait of King Louis XIV displayed at *The Forbidden City and the Palace of Versailles* exhibition.

Emperor Kangxi. Among them, Joachim Bouvet and Jean-Francois Gerbillon stayed to serve the Qing royal court. Across the following century, the two countries conducted extensive exchanges in areas like politics, economics, science and technology, culture, and arts.

The Forbidden City and the Palace of Versailles both bore witness to historical events of exchanges between China and France while acting as symbols of their respective cultures. In contemporary times, they are continuing efforts to foster exchanges and mutual learning between the two countries.

The Palace of Versailles and the Palace Museum have cooperated to hold an exhibition on Emperor Kangxi and an exhibition on King Louis XIV consecutively. The exhibition *The Forbidden City and the Palace of Versailles* marked a new starting point for exchanges and cooperation between the Palace Museum and French cultural institutions.

中国古代朝代对照简表

时代/王朝	起止时间
五帝	约前30世纪初—约前21世纪初
夏	约前2070—约前1600年
商	前1600—前1046年
周	前1046—前256年
西周	前1046—前771年
东周	前770—前256年
春秋	前770—前476年
战国	前475—前221年
秦	前221—前206年
汉	前206—220年
西汉	前206—25年
东汉	25—220年
三国	220—280年
魏	220—265年
蜀	221—263年
吴	222—280年
晋	265—420年
西晋	265—317年
东晋	317—420年

CHRONOLOGY OF ANCIENT CHINESE HISTORY

Period / Dynasty	Time Span
Period of the Five Legendary Rulers	c. early 30th century B.C.- c. early 21st century B.C.
Xia Dynasty	c. 2070-1600 B.C.
Shang Dynasty	1600-1046 B.C.
Zhou Dynasty	1046-256 B.C.
Western Zhou Dynasty	1046-771 B.C.
Eastern Zhou Dynasty	770-256 B.C.
Spring and Autumn Period	770-476 B.C.
Warring States Period	475-221 B.C.
Qin Dynasty	221-206 B.C.
Han Dynasty	206 B.C.-A.D. 220
Western Han Dynasty	206 B.C.-A.D. 25
Eastern Han Dynasty	A.D. 25-220
Three Kingdoms	220-280
Kingdom of Wei	220-265
Kingdom of Shu	221-263
Kingdom of Wu	222-280
Jin Dynasty	265-420
Western Jin Dynasty	265-317
Eastern Jin Dynasty	317-420

时代/王朝	起止时间
南北朝	420—589年
南朝	420—589年
北朝	386—581年
隋	581—618年
唐	618—907年
五代十国	907—960年
宋	960—1279年
北宋	960—1127年
南宋	1127—1279年
辽	907—1125年
西夏	1038—1227年
金	1115—1234年
元	1206—1368年
明	1368—1644年
清	1616—1911年

Period / Dynasty	Time Span
Northern and Southern Dynasties	420-589
Southern Dynasties	420-589
Northern Dynasties	386-581
Sui Dynasty	581-618
Tang Dynasty	618-907
Five Dynasties and Ten Kingdoms	907-960
Song Dynasty	960-1279
Northern Song Dynasty	960-1127
Southern Song Dynasty	1127-1279
Liao Dynasty	907-1125
Xixia Dynasty	1038-1227
Jin Dynasty	1115-1234
Yuan Dynasty	1206-1368
Ming Dynasty	1368-1644
Qing Dynasty	1616-1911

明清宫廷世系

明朝

年号 + 皇帝	本名	在位时间	生卒时间
洪武皇帝	朱元璋	1368—1398 年	1328—1398 年
建文皇帝	朱允炆	1399—1402 年	1377—1402 年
永乐皇帝	朱棣	1403—1424 年	1360—1424 年
洪熙皇帝	朱高炽	1425—1425 年	1378—1425 年
宣德皇帝	朱瞻基	1426—1435 年	1399—1435 年
正统皇帝	朱祁镇	1436—1449 年	1427—1464 年
景泰皇帝	朱祁钰	1450—1457 年	1428—1457 年
天顺皇帝	朱祁镇	1457—1464 年	1427—1464 年
成化皇帝	朱见深	1465—1487 年	1447—1487 年
弘治皇帝	朱祐樘	1488—1505 年	1470—1505 年
正德皇帝	朱厚照	1506—1521 年	1491—1521 年
嘉靖皇帝	朱厚熜	1522—1566 年	1507—1567 年
隆庆皇帝	朱载垕	1567—1572 年	1537—1572 年
万历皇帝	朱翊钧	1573—1620 年	1563—1620 年
泰昌皇帝	朱常洛	1620—1620 年	1582—1620 年
天启皇帝	朱由校	1621—1627 年	1605—1627 年
崇祯皇帝	朱由检	1628—1644 年	1611—1644 年

MING AND QING IMPERIAL LINEAGES

Ming Dynasty

Reign Title	Name	Reign Duration	Years of Birth and Death
Emperor Hongwu	Zhu Yuanzhang	1368-1398	1328-1398
Emperor Jianwen	Zhu Yunwen	1399-1402	1377-1402
Emperor Yongle	Zhu Di	1403-1424	1360-1424
Emperor Hongxi	Zhu Gaochi	1425-1425	1378-1425
Emperor Xuande	Zhu Zhanji	1426-1435	1399-1435
Emperor Zhengtong	Zhu Qizhen	1436-1449	1427-1464
Emperor Jingtai	Zhu Qiyu	1450-1457	1428-1457
Emperor Tianshun	Zhu Qizhen	1457-1464	1427-1464
Emperor Chenghua	Zhu Jianshen	1465-1487	1447-1487
Emperor Hongzhi	Zhu Youcheng	1488-1505	1470-1505
Emperor Zhengde	Zhu Houzhao	1506-1521	1491-1521
Emperor Jiajing	Zhu Houcong	1522-1566	1507-1567
Emperor Longqing	Zhu Zaihou	1567-1572	1537-1572
Emperor Wanli	Zhu Yijun	1573-1620	1563-1620
Emperor Taichang	Zhu Changluo	1620-1620	1582-1620
Emperor Tianqi	Zhu Youjiao	1621-1627	1605-1627
Emperor Chongzhen	Zhu Youjian	1628-1644	1611-1644

清朝

年号＋皇帝	本名	在位时间	生卒时间
	爱新觉罗·努尔哈赤	1616—1626 年	1559—1626 年
	爱新觉罗·皇太极	1626—1643 年	1592—1643 年
顺治皇帝	爱新觉罗·福临	1644—1661 年	1638—1661 年
康熙皇帝	爱新觉罗·玄烨	1662—1722 年	1654—1722 年
雍正皇帝	爱新觉罗·胤禛	1723—1735 年	1678—1735 年
乾隆皇帝	爱新觉罗·弘历	1736—1795 年	1711—1799 年
嘉庆皇帝	爱新觉罗·颙琰	1796—1820 年	1760—1820 年
道光皇帝	爱新觉罗·旻宁	1821—1850 年	1782—1850 年
咸丰皇帝	爱新觉罗·奕詝	1851—1861 年	1831—1861 年
同治皇帝	爱新觉罗·载淳	1862—1874 年	1856—1875 年
光绪皇帝	爱新觉罗·载湉	1875—1908 年	1871—1908 年
宣统皇帝	爱新觉罗·溥仪	1909—1911 年	1906—1967 年

Qing Dynasty

Reign Title	Name	Reign Duration	Years of Birth and Death
	Aisin Gioro Nurhaci	1616-1626	1559-1626
	Aisin Gioro Huang Taiji	1626-1643	1592-1643
Emperor Shunzhi	Aisin Gioro Fulin	1644-1661	1638-1661
Emperor Kangxi	Aisin Gioro Xuanye	1662-1722	1654-1722
Emperor Yongzheng	Aisin Gioro Yinzhen	1723-1735	1678-1735
Emperor Qianlong	Aisin Gioro Hongli	1736-1795	1711-1799
Emperor Jiaqing	Aisin Gioro Yongyan	1796-1820	1760-1820
Emperor Daoguang	Aisin Gioro Minning	1821-1850	1782-1850
Emperor Xianfeng	Aisin Gioro Yizhu	1851-1861	1831-1861
Emperor Tongzhi	Aisin Gioro Zaichun	1862-1874	1856-1875
Emperor Guangxu	Aisin Gioro Zaitian	1875-1908	1871-1908
Emperor Xuantong	Aisin Gioro Puyi	1909-1911	1906-1967

词条音序排列表

ENTRIES IN ALPHABETICAL ORDER

故宫建筑全景示意图

A PANORAMIC MAP OF THE PALACE MUSEUM

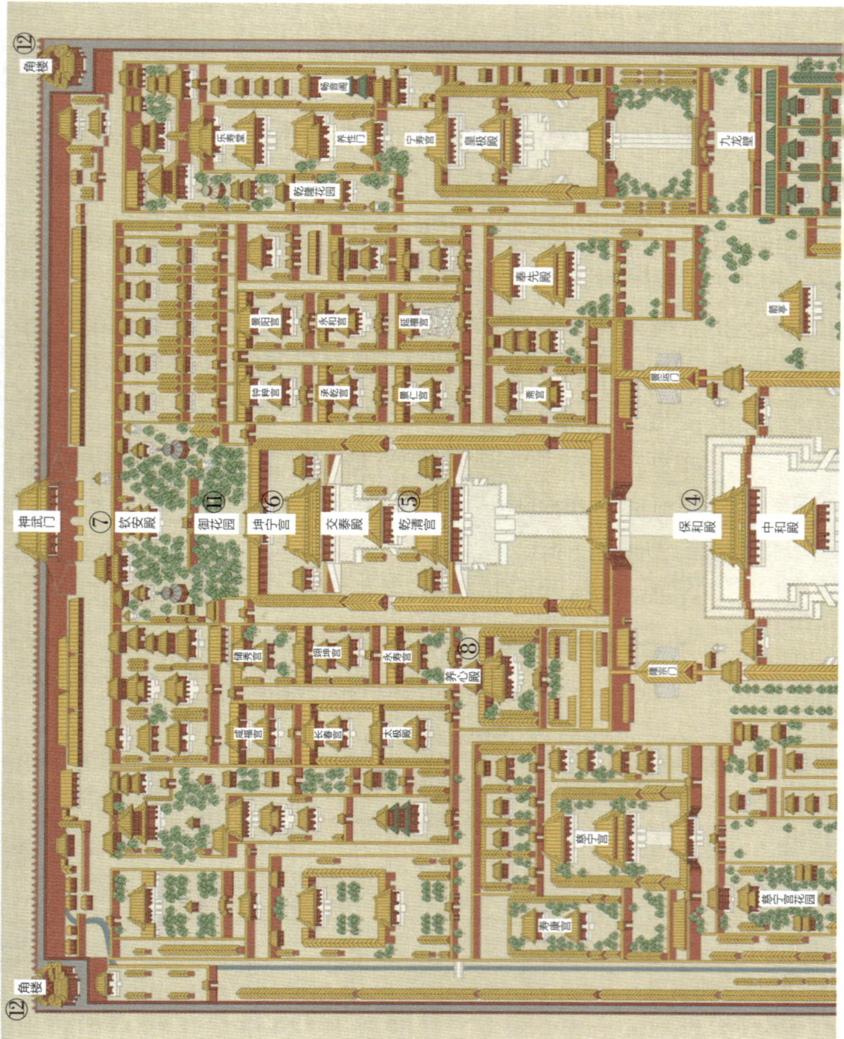

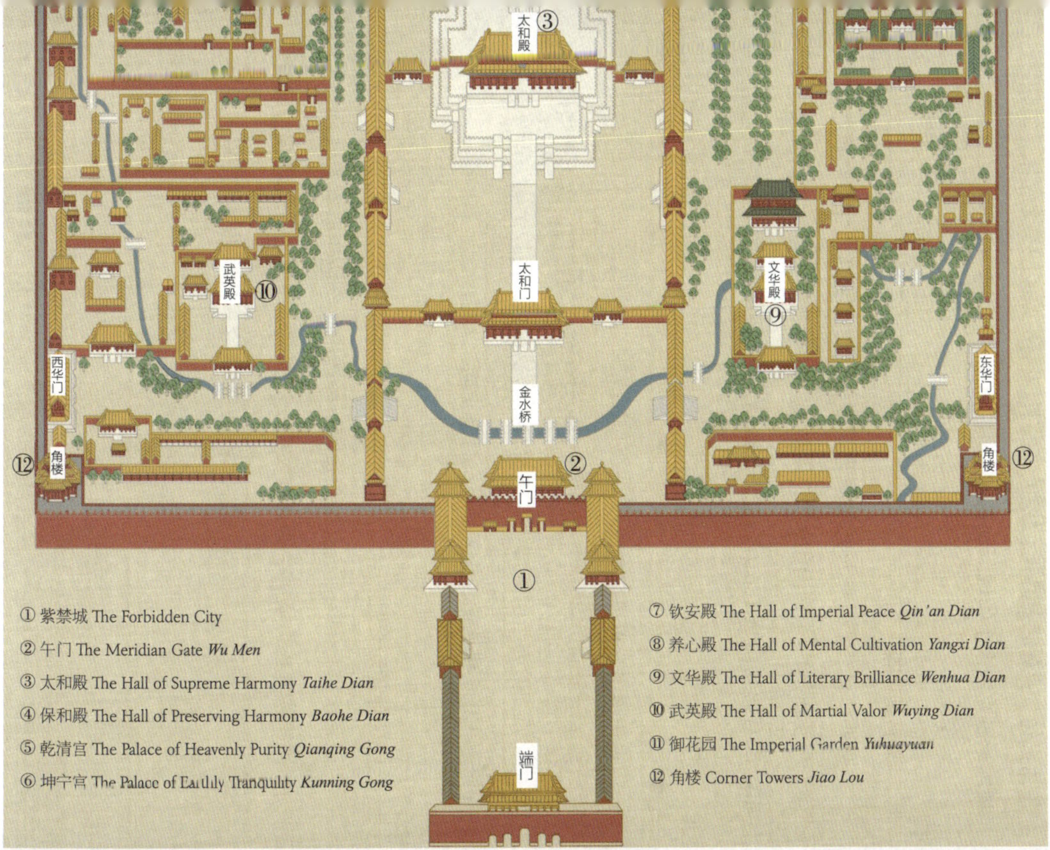
太和殿 ③
太和门
金水桥
午门 ②
①
端门
武英殿 ⑩
文华殿 ⑨
西华门
东华门
⑫ 角楼
角楼 ⑫
① 紫禁城 The Forbidden City
② 午门 The Meridian Gate *Wu Men*
③ 太和殿 The Hall of Supreme Harmony *Taihe Dian*
④ 保和殿 The Hall of Preserving Harmony *Baohe Dian*
⑤ 乾清宫 The Palace of Heavenly Purity *Qianqing Gong*
⑥ 坤宁宫 The Palace of Earthly Tranquility *Kunning Gong*
⑦ 钦安殿 The Hall of Imperial Peace *Qin'an Dian*
⑧ 养心殿 The Hall of Mental Cultivation *Yangxi Dian*
⑨ 文华殿 The Hall of Literary Brilliance *Wenhua Dian*
⑩ 武英殿 The Hall of Martial Valor *Wuying Dian*
⑪ 御花园 The Imperial Garden *Yuhuayuan*
⑫ 角楼 Corner Towers *Jiao Lou*

中国外文出版发行事业局

又称中国国际传播集团，是中国历史最悠久、规模最大的专业对外传播机构，业务涵盖翻译、出版、印刷、发行、互联网与多媒体、国际传播理论研究等多个领域，业务布局覆盖全球主要国家和地区。

故宫博物院

以明清皇宫紫禁城及其收藏为基础建立的大型综合性博物馆。故宫是世界文化遗产，是中国现存规模最大、保存最为完整的古代宫殿建筑群。故宫博物院藏 186 万余件 / 套藏品，堪称最重要的中国古代艺术宝库。

当代中国与世界研究院

国家专业智库机构，以应用研究和对策研究为特色，致力于当代中国与世界、讲好中国故事、翻译与对外话语体系、国际传播、世界舆情等研究工作，隶属中国外文出版发行事业局。

中国翻译研究院

国家级翻译智库平台，以翻译和对外话语体系应用研究为特色，致力于国家翻译能力研究、翻译与文明交流研究、重大对外翻译项目策划实施、高端翻译人才培养、跨文化交流合作等工作，隶属中国外文出版发行事业局。

China International Communications Group

China International Communications Group (CICG) is China's oldest and largest publisher with an international focus. Spanning all continents, its business covers translation, publishing, printing, distribution, and Internet and multimedia content. It also engages in research on issues related to cross-cultural communication.

The Palace Museum

The Palace Museum is a comprehensive museum based on the Forbidden City, the imperial palace of the Ming and Qing dynasties, and its collection. A World Cultural Heritage site, the Forbidden City is the largest and best-preserved ancient palace complex in China. It houses more than 1.86 million pieces (sets) of relics, making it the most important treasure house of ancient Chinese art.

Academy of Contemporary China and World Studies

As indicated by its name, Academy of Contemporary China and World Studies (ACCWS) is a national think-tank dedicated to research and policy planning focusing on contemporary China and the rest of the world. In addition to exploring effective ways to make China's stories reach an international audience, it also studies translation and interpretation, international discourse, cross-cultural communication, and global media opinions. It is affiliated with the China International Communications Group.

China Academy of Translation

China Academy of Translation (CATL) is a national think tank devoted to the study of translation, interpretation, and international discourse. Its mission is to conduct research on China's translation capacity and on the role of translation in cultural exchanges, coordinate national translation projects, organize advanced translator training, and promote cross-cultural communication and cooperation. It is affiliated with the China International Communications Group.

国审字（2025）第 00327 号

图书在版编目（CIP）数据

中国关键词 . 文物与文化遗产篇. 故宫：汉英对照 /
中国外文出版发行事业局等著 . -- 北京：朝华出版社，
2025. 5. -- ISBN 978-7-5054-5623-5
Ⅰ . D616；K928.74
中国国家版本馆 CIP 数据核字第 2025C9720M 号

中国关键词

文物与文化遗产篇 ♦ 汉英对照

故宫

KEYWORDS TO UNDERSTAND CHINA

Cultural Artifacts and Heritage

The Palace Museum

作　　者　中国外文出版发行事业局　故宫博物院　当代中国与世界研究院　中国翻译研究院
英文翻译　刘海乐
英文改稿　苏　格［美］
顾　　问　林东威
英文审定　王冬梅
特约编辑 / 项目执行　华光灿
项目管理　朱文博
责任编辑　赵　倩　张北鱼
责任印制　陆竞赢　訾　坤
书籍设计　晶　田
排版制作　创世禧图文
出版发行　朝华出版社
社　　址　北京西城区百万庄大街 24 号　邮政编码　100037
出版合作　（010）68995532
联系版权　zhbq@cicg.org.cn
网　　址　http: //zhcb.cicg.org.cn
印　　刷　天津中印联印务有限公司
经　　销　全国新华书店
开　　本　880mm × 1230mm 1/32
字　　数　124 千字
印　　张　8.5
版　　次　2025 年 5 月第 1 版 2025 年 5 月第 1 次印刷
装　　别　平
书　　号　ISBN 978-7-5054-5623-5
定　　价　98.00 元